What the Saints Never Said

What the Saints *Never* Said

Pious Misquotes
and the
Subtle Heresies
They Teach You

TRENT HORN

Catholic Answers Press

Published by
Catholic Answers, Inc.
2020 Gillespie Way
El Cajon, California 92020
1-888-291-8000 orders
619-387-0042 fax
catholic.com

Printed in the United States of America

Cover design by Theodore Schluenderfritz
Interior design by Claudine Mansour Design

978-1-68357-069-1
978-1-68357-070-7 Kindle
978-1-68357-071-4 ePub

To the saints:
pray for us.

Contents

Acknowledgments

THIS WORK WOULD not have been possible without the help of the Catholic Answers editorial department. In addition, I'm grateful to those who have researched these quotations before me and have included citations in their works. I know that some of these researchers might take me to task and find, for example, the original source for a quote that I have declared a fake. Great! If I can spur someone to provide a contribution to the collective wisdom of the saints, even if it is just a proper citation for that wisdom, then that is worth an emendation in a future edition of this book. As Cardinal Newman said, "Nothing would be done at all, if a man waited till he could do it so well that no one could find fault with it."[1]

Introduction

The villain clad in black raises his fist at the hero and says, "Luke, I am your father!" The dashing captain unfolds his communicator and gives the order, "Beam me up, Scotty." A mysterious jungle man sets down the woman he's rescued and she teaches him to say, "Me Tarzan, you Jane." What do these three things have in common?

You might say they're lines from famous movies: *The Empire Strikes Back*, *Star Trek*, and *Tarzan the Ape Man* respectively. But then you remembered this is a book about fake quotations and you changed your answer: they're misquotations from famous movies.

In *The Empire Strikes Back*, Luke Skywalker accuses Darth Vader of killing his father. Vader responds, "No, I am your father"—not "Luke, I am your father." The crew of the Starship Enterprise often asked Chief Engineer Montgomery Scott to beam them up via the transporter, but no one in the Star Trek films or television shows ever said, "Beam me up, Scotty."[2] Finally, in the 1932 classic *Tarzan the Ape Man*, Tarzan only says "Tarzan. Jane. Tarzan. Jane," not "Me Tarzan, you Jane."

Misquotations aren't restricted to fictional characters, either. George Washington never admitted to chopping down a cherry tree by saying, "I cannot tell a lie"; Albert Einstein never said, "Insanity is doing the same thing over and over again and expecting different results"; and Vince Lombardi didn't coin the phrase, "Winning isn't everything, it's the only thing."[3] In this book you'll see which famous sayings attributed to the saints of the Catholic faith are misquotations, misattributions, and in some cases total fabrications.

What's the Big Deal?

Before I continue, I need to address readers who might be rolling their eyes or muttering the word "nitpicker." Does it really matter if people get one word wrong in a line from a Star Wars film? Who cares if the cute story about George Washington and the cherry tree never happened? Why can't you just leave the saints alone and write about something important? But accurately recording the wisdom of saints and other well-known Catholics is important because truth is important.

We are ambassadors for Christ and our testimony about him needs to be trustworthy (2 Cor. 5:20). If people see us carelessly passing along information or stories that aren't true, then they may doubt us when we quote the wisdom of Christ or tell the story of salvation that has taken place through him. As St. Teresa of Avila once said, "Never affirm anything unless you are sure it is true."[4]

It's also important to give credit where credit is due. Imagine that your daughter broke a sports record and a friend of yours mistakenly praised your *son* for breaking that record. You'd gently remind this friend that it was actually your daughter's accomplishment, not your son's, because you'd want her to receive the praise she deserves for her hard work. Likewise, the saints are our brothers and sisters in Christ, and so we should do our best to accurately praise their wisdom and deeds that lead people closer to our Lord.

But the most important reason we should challenge false quotes from saints is because in some cases they contradict the Faith these saints embraced. I wouldn't be surprised if some of the saints are charitably yelling from heaven, "No! I actually said the opposite of that!" The major fake quotes in this book are not merely paraphrases of saintly wisdom or harmless pieces of advice that have been falsely attributed to the saints, although I do cover those kinds of quotes, too. Instead, each chapter in this book addresses a theme embodied in a well-known quote that is contrary to our Faith.

Part I addresses quotes that misunderstand the relationship between faith and works. They teach lessons like "Don't talk about Jesus with other people," "Good works matter more than being holy," and "Rely on yourself before you rely on God." Part II covers quotes that misunderstand the relationship between faith and reason and teach lessons like "Don't worry about defending the Faith," "God always wants you to be happy," and "Faith is belief apart from reason."

Tracking Down Fake Quotes

Most people come across fake quotes on popular quote websites or see them in online "memes" that contain pictures of famous people next to inspirational quotes. My favorite one of these memes has a picture of Abraham Lincoln next to this text: "The problem with quotes on the Internet is that it is hard to verify their authenticity."

Writing this book has shown me, however, that it is easier to prove an authentic quote than disprove an inauthentic quote.

To prove a quote is authentic, you only have to produce the work from which the quote comes. In some cases, the person to whom the quote is attributed may not have left behind any writings, and so a citation from a reliable secondary source can suffice. For example, during his earthly ministry Jesus did not write anything down, so the record of what he said is recorded in the Gospels. But even these are not exhaustive. St. Paul, for example, recites a saying of Jesus' that is not recorded in the Gospels: "It is more blessed to give than to receive" (Acts 20:35). St. John tells us that "there are also many other things which Jesus did; were every one of them to be written, I suppose that the world itself could not contain the books that would be written" (John 21:25).

This leads to the problem of proving that a certain quote is inauthentic. What John says about Jesus is true, generally speaking, about most people. People say and do much more than what is recorded about them in biographies or even their own autobiographies and memoirs. Therefore, when I say that a certain quote is inauthentic or fake, I'm not saying it is certain the person never uttered the words in question. Instead, I'm saying that we have no reason to believe they said these words because they do not exist in either a primary source or a reliable secondary source that describes what he or she said and did.

In some cases, a disputed quote contains evidence of its own inauthenticity through a contradiction or anachronism. For example, the Irish author Oscar Wilde is reputed to have said, "You don't love someone for their looks, or their clothes, or for their fancy car, but because they sing a song only you can hear." But Wilde died three years before the Ford Motor Company produced the Model A, much less any kind of "fancy car." Moreover, he described cars in 1900, the year of his death, as "nervous, irritable, strange things," so it's doubtful he'd speak well of automobiles in general.[5]

When it comes to famous saint quotes, some of them may not appear in any of the saint's extant writings or in any early secondary sources, or may contain similar anachronisms or may contradict something in the saint's authentic writings, thus showing the quote in question is not authentic. An allegedly original saying found in the earlier writings of another person becomes proof of the quote's true origin. A slam-dunk case for inauthenticity would include all three elements: absence in primary and secondary sources, anachronism/contradiction, and attribution to another author.

What Makes a Saint Quote Fake?

The kinds of fake quotes that are attributed to the saints come in roughly one of three types: misquotes, misattributions, and fabrications.

A misquote (or what I call "close, but not quite") is similar to something a saint did say but still different enough to warrant mentioning. The earlier example from *The Empire Strikes Back* is a classic example of a misquotation; the real quote and the misquote differ by only one word. These kinds of misquotes are usually just harmless paraphrases, but in some cases changing one word in a passage can alter the entire meaning.

A misattribution occurs when an authentic quote is attributed to someone who did not originate it. For example, many people think the famous circus owner P.T. Barnum said, "There's a sucker born every minute," but Barnum was too shrewd to insult the public so blatantly (Barnum did say people could be easily "humbugged," or duped).[6] Likelier candidates for the quote include Barnum's rival Adam Forepaugh, and con man Joseph Bessimer."[7]

A fabrication is essentially a quote that has no original source. These usually appear in the form of anonymous, inspirational quotes that are attached to famous people in order to make them sound more impressive. Even though they are fabrications, I doubt the majority of them are intentional deceptions.

A person may have come across an anonymous piece of wisdom and falsely believed it to come from a famous person or heard someone else attribute it to that person. When I give a specific verdict on these quotes I usually say they are probably fake because it is difficult to prove beyond any doubt that a person did not say something. The only instances when I say a quote is clearly fake are when they contain obvious anachronisms or are incorrectly attributed to the Bible, since Scripture can be exhaustively searched in a way quotations outside of Scripture cannot.

Now that I've defined what I mean by the term "fake," I should also elaborate on what I mean by the term "saint." In this book, "saint" loosely refers to any famous Catholic. Most of the people I discuss are canonized saints, but others include popes, early Catholic writers, Catholic historical figures, and even the Bible. Fake saint quotes, for my purposes, are inauthentic quotations that are popular in the Catholic community but are incorrectly attributed to a Catholic source.

I don't wish to imply that people who believe in the authenticity of a fake saint quote are gullible or unintelligent. No one has time to research every fact or quote they hear or read, so we do our best to judge if something sounds right and hope our judgment pans out. I used to say, "Fake quotes and misinformation can spread quickly because, as Mark Twain said, 'A lie can get half-way around the world before the truth has time to put it's shoes on.'" But it turns out that line came from the Irish satirist Jonathan Swift, so I understand that anyone can make a mistake in these matters.[7]

Finally, I must express my gratitude to the Lord for inspiring so many holy men and women to impart their God-given wisdom to us in their writings and personal lives. It is my hope that this research will make it easier to learn the genuine wisdom of the saints and, in doing so, imitate them as they imitate Christ (cf. 1 Cor. 11:1). Pope St. Clement put it well, "Cleave to the holy [saints], for those that cleave to them shall [themselves] be made holy [saints]."[9]

What the Saints Never Said

PART I

Faith
and
Works

1. "Preach the gospel always; if necessary, use words."

—ST. FRANCIS OF ASSISI?

WHEN I TOLD people I was writing a book about fake saint quotes their first response was always, "Oh, you mean like, 'Preach the gospel always; if necessary, use words.'" You hear this quote in untold numbers of Catholic schools and churches in spite of the fact that many people, including historians, know it's not authentic. Mark Galli, the author of *Francis of Assisi and His World*, says of this saying, "No biography written within the first 200 years of [Francis's] death contains the saying. It's not likely that a pithy quote like this would have been missed by his earliest disciples."[10]

The oldest source I have found for it is Daisy Osborne's 1990 book *Woman without Limits*. She describes (without citing any sources) how St. Francis and his disciples once went into a village to preach the gospel but instead of preaching they ended up "showing love to the needy, friendship to the lonely, and compassion to the unfortunate." When one of the disciples lamented that "not a single sermon [had] been delivered," Francis allegedly replied, "Oh, but yes! We have been preaching the gospel the whole day."[11]

Another clue that this saying is from the 1990s comes from a blog post by Fr. Pat McCloskey, the Franciscan editor of *St. Anthony Messenger*. He says, "I had been a Franciscan for 28 years—and had earned an M.A. in Franciscan studies—before I heard the 'if necessary, use words' quote. That was during Msgr. Kenneth Velo's homily at Cardinal Joseph L.

Bernardin's funeral in 1996."[12]

Many of the books that cite this quote admit it is spurious but justify quoting or even attributing it to St. Francis of Assisi because its message is still "Franciscan" in nature. Gary Krause writes in his book *God's Great Missionaries*, "There's no evidence that Saint Francis actually made this statement, but it certainly fits the spirit of his teachings."[13] But this quote only reflects "the spirit of St. Francis" if we 1) misunderstand the person of St. Francis, and 2) misinterpret the meaning of this apocryphal saying.

Words Aren't Optional Accessories

Let's start with the quote itself. Most people think it means "Preach the gospel in word and deed," or "Live the gospel that you preach." If that were true, then it would be similar to Mother Teresa's declaration, "Joy is a net of love in which you can catch souls."[14] If the quote meant, "You can evangelize with good deeds as well as words," then I could tolerate it, even though it's not authentic. But two words complicate this interpretation—"if necessary." Preach the gospel always; *if necessary,* use words.

Consider this advice: "Love your spouse. Use words if necessary." Most spouses would appreciate receiving acts of service and affectionate gifts, but they would still be hurt if they never heard the words "I love you." Or imagine if I told you, "Build a fire. Use wood if necessary." You would probably assume I meant, "Use wood as a last resort," or "It would be great if you could build the fire without wood."

Words are not an inferior tool we use to share the gospel when actions won't suffice. Words are to the preaching of the gospel as wood is to the building of a fire; the latter cannot be done well without the former. Sure, you could burn fabric to make a fire, but it wouldn't be as effective as firewood. And you might be able to present our faith through actions alone, but it wouldn't be as effective as carefully chosen words that describe the Gospel that is, "the power of God that brings salvation to everyone who has faith" (Rom. 1:16).

"All the darkness in the world cannot extinguish the light of a single candle."
—ST. FRANCIS OF ASSISI?

The earliest citations of this quote come from the 1970s and do not mention St. Francis. The oldest I found was an opening prayer offered by the Reverend Wilbur C. Christians at a 1972 California Senate meeting. It makes no mention of St. Francis. It is addressed to "Almighty Creative Spirit," and ends, "We pray, in faith, and hope, and love, confident that all the darkness in the world cannot extinguish the light of a single candle."[15]

St. John tells us that Jesus is "the light of men. The light shines in the darkness, and the darkness has not overcome it" (John 1:5). In a similar vein St. Paul says of us, "Once you were darkness, but now you are light in the Lord; walk as children of light" (Eph. 5:8).

It's true that extraordinary acts of charity can make people more receptive to the gospel. This was especially the case when Christian morality stood in contrast to barbaric customs among those being evangelized. For example, the second-century letter to Diognetus says that Christians "beget children; but they do not destroy their offspring. They have a common table, but not a common bed [meaning they don't swap wives]. They are in the flesh, but they do not live after the flesh."[16]

Christians in ancient Rome not only refrained from committing abortion or infanticide, they rescued infants whose parents had abandoned them. The Roman emperor Julian the Apostate complained that Christians "support not only their own poor but ours as well; all men see that our people lack aid from us."[17]

Christians also created the first hospitals for the poor, and it was considered a mark of holiness to expose oneself to disease in order to care for the sick. An example of this heroism can be seen in St. Damien of Molokai, who cared for the lepers of Hawaii until he died from leprosy. He said, "I make myself a leper with the lepers to gain all to Jesus Christ."[18]

Thankfully, the Church's witness has gradually expelled pagan darkness, and now one third of the world identifies as Christian and half claim to worship the God of Abraham. In developing parts of the world, Christian charity and rejection of barbarisms like child marriage or honor killing allow actions that communicate the gospel to some degree. But in more developed, nominally Christian areas of the West, it is common to find people who understand the value of loving their fellow man but do not understand how this relates to Christianity, which they see as just a bunch of arbitrary rules about morality, and especially sexual morality.

Good deeds alone can't communicate the Christian faith to these people because many other religious and nonreligious people perform similar acts of charity and kindness. Instead, good deeds must be accompanied by words and attitudes that are, as St. Paul said, "not ashamed of the gospel: it is the power of God for salvation to everyone who has faith" (Rom. 1:17).

Have You Heard the Word?

One reason I think people seek to "preach with actions" instead of words is because they live in a culture that is averse to Christian preaching. If a movie is "preachy," that means it has an obnoxious, self-righteous tone. When many people think of "preachers" they think of men who callously shout at the top of their lungs about fire, brimstone, and damnation.

In the classic film *Inherit the Wind*, the Reverend Jeremiah Brown says of local schoolteacher Bertram Cates, "Do we call down hellfire on the man who has sinned against the Word? . . . Strike down this sinner, as Thou didst Thine enemies of old, in the days of the Pharaohs!"[19]

"To convert somebody go and take them by the hand and guide them."
—ST. THOMAS AQUINAS?

An Internet search only shows this quote on popular quote websites and in books written in the twenty-first century, which we would not expect with an authentic quote from the *Summa Theologiae*. A similar passage in the *Summa* may have served as an inspiration for it: "Angels are appointed to the guardianship of men, that they may take them by the hand and guide them to eternal life, encourage them to good works, and protect them against the assaults of the demons."[20]

Such an aversion may be warranted for bad preaching, but it doesn't apply to good forms of preaching like those we find in Scripture. Jesus was an itinerant preacher who was so good that he attracted crowds of people who were "astonished" at what he said (Matt. 7:28). After he heard that John the Baptist had been arrested, Matthew tells us, "Jesus began to preach, saying, 'Repent, for the kingdom of heaven is at hand'" (Matt 4:17). When a crowd of people wanted Jesus to stay with them he declined, saying, "I must preach the good news of the kingdom of God to the other cities also; for I was sent for this purpose" (Luke 4:43).

St. Peter says that after the Resurrection Jesus commanded the apostles "to preach to the people, and to testify that he is the one ordained by God to be judge of the living and the dead" (Acts 10:42). When Peter preached the first sermon in the history of the Church, a crowd in Jerusalem was "cut to the heart" when he convinced them of their culpability for Jesus' death (Acts 2:37). Peter then encouraged them to repent, and as a result, "those who received his word were baptized, and there were added that day about three thousand souls (Acts 2:41).

We aren't all called to preach the gospel by giving a public address to a crowd of strangers. But we can all share the gospel by describing what Christ has done for humanity as a whole and for each of us as individuals. People won't accuse you of being preachy if you follow the advice Paul gave to the Christians in Colossae: "Let your speech always be gracious, seasoned with salt, so that you may know how you ought to answer everyone" (Col. 4:6). There is even someone we can turn to as an example of how to preach about the difficult parts of our Faith like hell or sin—St. Francis of Assisi.

St. Francis the Preacher

When most people think of St. Francis they usually think of a hippie clad in brown robes who preached peace to an audience of wide-eyed animals from a Disney film. And although he was kind to animals and praised God for all of creation, this represents a modern, sentimental view of St. Francis. It completely glosses over the man who renounced his former, sinful life and wanted to preach Jesus Christ to others. Thomas of Celeno, who wrote the first biography of Francis, says, "His words were neither hollow nor ridiculous, but filled with the power of the Holy Spirit, penetrating the marrow of the heart, so that listeners were turned to great amazement."[21]

In Francis's time homiletic training at Europe's universities stressed scholarly acumen more than pastoral sensitivity. This resulted in sermons that were dry or harsh in tone, but Francis had not attended one of these universities so his preaching drew primarily from his conversion experience.[22] It was also vibrant and energetic, and it was common for Francis to sing and dance with joy and then openly weep when talking about God's mercy.[23]

Mark Galli says that Francis "imitated the troubadours, employing poetry and word pictures to drive the message home. When he described the Nativity, listeners felt as if Mary was giving birth before their eyes; in rehearsing the crucifixion, the crowd (as did Francis) would shed tears."[24] Francis himself said, "What are the servants of God if not his minstrels, who must move people's hearts and lift them up to spiritual joy?"[25]

Francis's focus on sharing the interior spiritual life can also be seen in this advice he gave other members of his order: "The preacher must first draw from secret prayers what he will later pour out in holy sermons; he must first grow hot within before he speaks words that are in themselves cold."[26] Ugolino Brunforte, who collected some of the earliest traditions about St. Francis, records what happened when he drew from this spiritual well while preaching in his hometown of Assisi:

> St. Francis ascended the pulpit, and began to preach in so wonderful a way on holy penance, on the world, on voluntary poverty, on the hope of life eternal, on the nakedness of Christ, on the shame of the Passion of our Blessed Savior, that all those who heard him, both men and women, began to weep bitterly, being moved to devotion and compunction; and in all Assisi the Passion of Christ was commemorated as it never had been before.[27]

One of the topics that Francis often preached about was the joy of repenting from sin. Far from being a "light and fluffy" new-ager, Francis did not mince words when it came to this subject. He writes, "Blessed are those who die in penance, for they shall be in the kingdom of heaven. Woe to those who do not die in penance, for they shall be children of the devil whose works they do and they shall go into everlasting fire."[28]

"When the devil reminds you of your past, remind him of his future!"
—ST. TERESA OF AVILA?

This is a common saying that was included in a book about saintly wisdom. One of that book's chapters refers to St. Teresa's *The Way of Perfection*, in which she said, "In order to disturb the soul and keep it from enjoying these great blessings, the devil will suggest to it a thousand false fears." She then encouraged her fellow nuns to pray for those who seemed to be blessed, because "No one can be safe in this life amid the engulfing dangers of this stormy sea."[29]

In *Saintly Solutions to Life's Common Problems*, Fr. Joseph Esper wrote, "St. Teresa of Avila reminds you that the devil will try to upset you by suggesting a thousand false fears . . . laugh at the absurdity of the situation: Satan, the epitome of sin itself, accuses you of unworthiness. Furthermore, as the saying goes [not a saying of St. Teresa], "When the devil reminds you of your past, remind him of his future!"[30]

Francis did not sugarcoat the reality of damnation, but he also preached the joy that comes from Christ liberating us from sin and its justly deserved punishments. He told his lay and religious followers, "O how holy and how loving, gratifying, humbling, peace-giving, sweet, worthy of love, and above all things desirable it is to have such a Brother and such a Son: our Lord Jesus Christ, Who laid down his life for his sheep."[31] He also gave them practical advice in the form of admonitions:

Where there is poverty and joy, there is neither greed nor avarice.

Where there is peace and meditation, there is neither anxiety nor doubt.

Where there is a heart full of mercy and discernment, there is neither excess nor hardness of heart.[32]

Preaching was so important to Francis that he required his religious brothers to get permission to do it. For those who could not formally preach, he encouraged them to "preach by their deeds," but this did not mean he thought evangelism should be restricted to public displays of good deeds.[33] After all, an unconverted person might see an example of piety that inspires him, but then doubt that God would love a "sinner" like him. This person doesn't just need an example of holiness; he needs encouraging words about God's transforming love for him (or the gospel), explained in a way he can understand.

St. Paul recognized the need for this preaching when he wrote the Christians in Rome a message that is just as true today as it was two thousand years ago. It is a message you should always bring up when someone suggests that you "preach the gospel" apart from words:

For, "everyone who calls upon the name of the Lord will be saved." But how are men to call upon him in whom they have not believed? And how are they to believe in him of whom they have never heard? And how are they to hear without a preacher? And how can men preach unless they are sent? As it is written, "How beautiful are the feet of those who preach good news!" (Rom. 10:13-15).

A Better Quote

"We must all try to be preachers by our deeds."
—ST. TERESA OF AVILA[34]

Notice that this quote does not say we should *only* preach with deeds or that we should add words to deeds if necessary. It's just a simple reminder that our actions can speak as loud as words so we should preach with our deeds just as we would preach with our words. Also, we should make sure what we preach with words matches what we preach in deed. Inconsistent Christians have been around since the beginning of the Church, as is evident in this fourth-century piece of advice from St. Jerome, "Do not let your deeds belie your words; lest when you speak in church someone may mentally reply, 'Why do you not practice what you profess?'"[35]

2. "People are illogical, unreasonable, and self-centered . . . Love them anyway."

—MOTHER TERESA?

DURING THE LATE 1960s British journalist Malcolm Muggeridge traveled the world filming religious documentaries for the BBC. His most famous was about a diminutive Albanian nun named Anjezë Gonxhe Bojaxhiu, or as the poor in Calcutta called her, Mother Teresa. Muggeridge's subsequent book and documentary, *Something Beautiful for God*, catapulted Mother Teresa onto the world stage. In the years that followed, she met with dozens of foreign leaders, received the Nobel Peace Prize, and even brokered a cease-fire during the 1982 Lebanon War.

Almost twenty years after her death in 1997, the Church approved Mother Teresa's canonization and she is now called St. Teresa of Calcutta, although many people, myself included, still affectionately refer to her as Mother Teresa. Her fame led to a collection of alleged Mother Teresa quotes that have become so popular that the Mother Teresa Center has a section on its website dedicated to exposing "quotes falsely attributed to Mother Teresa." While most of them are relatively harmless paraphrases of things Mother Teresa actually said, others misrepresent the beliefs of Calcutta's patron saint.

Helping Hands and Praying Lips

One night I was reading in my study when my wife handed me her phone and said, "My friend posted something ridiculous on Facebook. What should I say to her?" I looked down at the screen and saw that her friend had written, "I hate when Catholics get so hung up on rules. Just love other people! Mother Teresa said, 'Helping hands are better than praying lips.'"

"Did Mother Teresa really say that?" my wife nervously asked.

"I think it is very good when people suffer. To me, that is like the kiss of Jesus."
—MOTHER TERESA**?**

This appears to be an inaccurate paraphrase of the following excerpt from Mother Teresa's address at the 1994 National Prayer Breakfast: "One day I met a lady who was dying of cancer in a most terrible condition. And I told her, I say, 'You know, this terrible pain is only the kiss of Jesus—a sign that you have come so close to Jesus on the cross that he can kiss you.' And she joined her hands together and said, 'Mother Teresa, please tell Jesus to stop kissing me.'"[36]

I walked across the room and grabbed one of Mother Teresa's books off my shelf. "Given what she says about prayer in her writings, I highly doubt this is an authentic quote. Let me check it out." After a half hour of investigating I found the quote's true source: a nineteenth-century agnostic named Robert Ingersoll.

A Civil War veteran, skilled lawyer, and eloquent public speaker, some people believed Ingersoll could have run for president—if he weren't so opposed to religion.[37] His contemporaries called him "the Great Agnostic," and if Ingersoll were alive today he would probably have joined the ranks of "New Atheists" like Richard Dawkins. To give an example, during an 1899 speech at a benefit for a local charity, Ingersoll couldn't resist making the following jab at religious sensibilities, which over a hundred years later my wife's friend attributed to Mother Teresa:

> This is the work of the generous men and women who contribute to the Actors Fund. This is charity; and these generous men and women have taught, and are teaching, a lesson that all the world should learn, and that is this: The hands that help are holier than the lips that pray.[38]

Catholics don't believe we must choose between praying to God and doing good works. Instead, as we grow closer to God through prayer we become filled with his grace, and this empowers us to love others just as he has loved us (cf. 1 John 4:19). In fact, people who fail to do this show that they don't really love God, even though they claim to love him. According to St. John, "If any one says, 'I love God,' and hates his brother, he is a liar; he who does not love his brother whom he has seen, cannot love God whom he has not seen" (1 John 4:20).

Some studies have even shown that religious people are more likely to give to charity and volunteer their time than nonreligious people.[39] In other words, the hands that help often belong to people who pray. Mother Teresa expressed a similar sentiment, "[W]ithout God we are too poor to help the poor, but when we pray, God places his love in us. Look, the Sisters are poor, but they pray. The fruit of prayer is love. The fruit of love is service. Only when you pray can you really serve the poor."[40]

The Saddest Thing?

Some apocryphal Mother Teresa quotes portray her as a woman who valued good works over acts of faith, but the following quote does the opposite. You can find this alleged confession from Mother Teresa on some websites critical of changes made to the liturgy after the Second Vatican Council: "The thing that makes me saddest is watching people receive Communion in the hand."

The source of the quote is Fr. George Rutler, who is said to have preached a homily in New York in 1989 in which he recounted speaking with Mother Teresa. He claimed that after celebrating Mass with the Missionaries of Charity, he asked Mother Teresa, "What do you think is the worst problem in the world today?" Fr. Rutler then said in his homily:

> She more than anyone could name any number of candidates: famine, plague, disease, the breakdown of the family, rebellion against God, the corruption of the media, world debt, nuclear threat, and so on. Without pausing a second she said, "Wherever I go in the whole world, the thing that makes me the saddest is watching people receive Communion in the hand."[41]

There are several reasons to doubt Mother Teresa said this. First, if receiving Communion in the hand upset Mother Teresa more than evils like poverty or abortion, then why didn't she *publicly* denounce reception of Communion in the hand as much as she denounced, for example, abortion, which she called "the greatest destroyer of peace today".[42]

"The fruit of abortion is nuclear war."
—MOTHER TERESA**?**

No reliable source records Mother Teresa making a connection between abortion and nuclear war, and the Mother Teresa Center considers this quote to be spurious. However, Mother Teresa did say at the 1994 National Prayer Breakfast, "if we accept that a mother can kill even her own child, how can we tell other people not to kill one another?"[43]

Second, the Mother Teresa Center says, "This statement does not seem authentic to us. We have never heard Mother Teresa saying these words nor read them in her writings . . . Mother Teresa would not have contradicted the Church."[44] Finally, in a 2016 article, Fr. Rutler clarified what Mother Teresa said to him decades earlier. Specifically, Mother Teresa said she was most sad when people received the Eucharist *irreverently* and not merely in the hand. He writes:

> She told me once after Mass that the "saddest thing in the world" was to watch people receiving the Blessed Sacrament irreverently. She motioned with her hands but she was speaking of the inward disposition of the soul and not the physical manner of Communion, whether in the hand or on the tongue. I mentioned this in a broadcast talk that was widely interpreted as Mother's disapproval of Communion in the hand. This distressed her since the bishops had conceded both forms.[45]

The Eucharist has been traditionally received on the tongue but there is nothing wrong with receiving it in the hand. The Vatican's Congregation for Divine Worship says that "if any communicant should wish to receive the Sacrament in the hand, in areas where the Bishops' Conference with the recognition of the Apostolic See has given permission, the sacred host is to be administered to him or her."[46] In the fourth century, St. Cyril of Jerusalem advised recent converts to the Faith that when they received Communion they ought to "make [their] left hand a throne for the right, as for that which is to receive a King."[47]

As long as we treat the King of Kings with reverence (which is what Mother Teresa was most concerned about), then it should not matter whether we receive him in our hands or in our mouths.

Three More Dubious Mother Teresa Quotes

1. "Live simply so others may simply live."

This quote has also been attributed to Gandhi and St. Elizabeth Ann Seton, but there is no specific citation that connects it to any famous person, including Mother Teresa.

2. "I have found the paradox that if I love until it hurts, then there is not hurt, but only more love."

This is a personal observation Daphne Rae made at the end of her 1981 book *Love Until It Hurts: The Work of Mother Teresa and Her Missionaries of Charity.*

3. "There is a light in this world. A healing spirit more powerful than any darkness we may encounter."

This comes from Richard Attenborough's opening narration of a 1986 documentary about Mother Teresa and not from anything she said or wrote herself.

"Love Them Anyway"

If you search "Mother Teresa poem" on the Internet you'll find one called "The Anyway Poem," which is attributed to her. Here's an excerpt:

> People are often unreasonable, illogical and self-centered;
>   Forgive them anyway.
>
> If you are kind, people may accuse you of selfish, ulterior motives;
>   Be kind anyway . . .
>
> Give the world the best you have, and it may never be enough;
>   Give the world the best you've got anyway.
>
> You see, in the final analysis, it is between you and God;
>   It was never between you and them anyway.

The poem is actually a modified version of Kent M. Keith's "Paradoxical Commandments," which he wrote in college in 1968.[48] "The Anyway Poem" contains most of Keith's commandments but in a slightly modified form. For example, Keith said, "People are illogical, unreasonable, and self-centered. Love them anyway," whereas "The Anyway Poem" says, "People are illogical, unreasonable, and self-centered. *Forgive them anyway* [emphasis added]." The final line of Keith's original commandments was, "Give the world the best you have and you'll get kicked in the teeth. Give the world the best you have anyway." It did not include the final line attributed to Mother Teresa, mentioning "God" and a "final analysis."

"Love is the condition in which the happiness of another person is essential to your own."
—MOTHER TERESA**?**

This comes from Robert Heinlein's 1961 science fiction novel, *Stranger in a Strange Land.* In one scene an older gentleman named Jubal asks a younger man named Ben, "What is love?" Ben replies, "Nobody has answered it yet. All I know is, it hurts." Jubal then says, "Love is that condition in which the happiness of another person is essential to your own."[49] Mother Teresa described the nature of love in this way: "For God so loved the world, so much, that he gave his Son [cf. John 3:16]. Love is a one-way street. It always moves away from self in the direction of the other. Love is the ultimate gift of our selves to others."[50]

The paradoxical commandments became associated with Mother Teresa after the publication of her 1995 book, *A Simple Path*, which contains eight of Keith's commandments with slight differences in wording. Underneath the commandments was a caption describing how they were found on "a sign on the wall of Shishu Bhavan, the children's home in Calcutta."[51]

A Simple Path did not attribute the poem to Mother Teresa, but it's easy to see how readers accidentally attributed it to her. In 1997, Keith heard his poem read aloud at a Rotary Club meeting and, after a trip to the library, he found it in *A Simple Path*. He writes:

I stood there in the bookstore, chills going up and down my spine. It was an incredible moment for me. Something I had written thirty years earlier had made its way around the world to India, where Mother Teresa or one of her coworkers had thought it important enough to put up on the wall, to look at every day as they ministered to their children. I was deeply moved.[52]

While Keith's original commandments contain helpful pieces of advice, the final lines of the Internet's "The Anyway Poem" are problematic: "You see, in the final analysis, it is between you and God/It was never between you and them anyway." Some versions even call the poem "The Final Analysis," but that could be interpreted to mean that Mother Teresa only helped the poor in order to gain favor with God at the final judgment. Keith is also critical of this addition to his work:

> Jesus said that there are two great commandments—to love God, and to love our neighbor as ourselves. So in the final analysis, it is between you and God, but it is also between you and "them." And when it comes to them, Jesus made it clear that we have to love people and help people anyway. We can't give up on them or ignore them or write them off. That is the point of the Paradoxical Commandments as well—we find meaning when we love and help people, no matter who they may be, or how difficult they may be. We find meaning by loving and helping them anyway.[53]

We aren't called to love other people just so that in some "final analysis" God will see we were charitable with illogical, selfish pests. Rather, God's grace saves us from being illogical, selfish pests, and it empowers us to see the image of God in every person and to love them accordingly.

CLOSE, BUT NOT QUITE

"Not all of us can do great things. But we can all do small things with great love."
—MOTHER TERESA**?**

I once fell for an apocryphal Mother Teresa quote when I told my classmates in a speech at my high school graduation, "Not all of us can do great things. But we can all do small things with great love." If I could go back I would have made a slight alteration and adapted this portion of Mother Teresa's 1979 Nobel Prize acceptance speech:

> There is so much suffering, so much hatred, so much misery, and we with our prayer, with our sacrifice are beginning at home. Love begins at home, and it is not how much we do, but how much love we put in the action that we do. It is to God Almighty—how much we do it does not matter, because he is infinite, but how much love we put in that action. How much we do to him in the person that we are serving.[54]

Nobody's a "Mother Teresa"

Some people think they can't make God the most important part of their life because they're no "Mother Teresa." They're just a regular person with all kinds of issues and struggles with sin. But Mother Teresa was not a pious robot. She faced the same struggles many believers face, including bouts of what St. John of the Cross called "the dark night of the soul."

Once during a retreat, Mother Teresa knelt before the Blessed Sacrament and asked a priest next to her, "Dear Father, pray for me. Where is Jesus?" That priest later described how Mother Teresa "frequently shared with [him] the spiritual dryness that accompanies her labors as a Missionary of Charity."[55] But rather than fall into despair and unbelief, Mother Teresa persevered in faith by remembering her true identity.

She was not someone who desired the limelight or wanted to become a philanthropic celebrity. The key to Mother Teresa's holiness lies not in what she did, but in remaining devoted to the Lord even when she felt far away from him. And it is that devotion we can all emulate no matter how burdened we feel by sin or anxiety in this life.

Who was Mother Teresa? She tells us, "By blood, I am Albanian. By citizenship, an Indian. By faith, I am a Catholic nun. As to my calling, I belong to the world. As to my heart, I belong entirely to the Heart of Jesus."[56]

A Better Quote

> *"Charity and devotion differ no more, the one from the other, than the flame from the fire."*
> —ST. FRANCIS DE SALES

Some people act like the different parts of our spiritual lives were separated from one another like watertight compartments on a ship. Prayer is something we do on mornings, evenings, and Sundays whereas charity is something we practice during the week to prove our prayers are authentic. But St. Francis de Sales taught that works of charity should not be done to vindicate our piety; they are instead the natural consequence of it. He writes,

> [S]ince devotion consists in a certain excelling degree of charity, it not only makes us ready, active, and diligent in observing all the commandments of God; but it also prompts us to do readily and heartily as many good works as we can, even though they be not in any sort commanded . . . Charity and devotion differ no more, the one from the other, than the flame from the fire; inasmuch as charity, being a spiritual fire, when it breaks out into flame, is called devotion.[57]

3. "You don't need to believe in God to be a good person."

—POPE FRANCIS?

AN ATHEIST COMMENTER on my Facebook page once said that even the pope disagreed with my "narrow views" on religion. He then posted a picture on his Facebook page of a grinning Pope Francis with the following words plastered next to him:

> It is not necessary to believe in God to be a good person. In a way, the traditional notion of God is outdated. One can be spiritual but not religious. It is not necessary to go to church and give money—for many, nature can be a church. Some of the best people in history do not believe in God, while some of the worst deeds were done in his name.

What I found most amusing about our exchange was that this atheist criticized believers for not "following the evidence." He crowed about how atheists follow a maxim coined by the late Carl Sagan: "Extraordinary claims require extraordinary evidence."[58] Yet he did not think his extraordinary claim about the pope's views on God and religion required even *ordinary* evidence, like a link to a reputable news source. Instead, he provided an easily debunked, fake quote.

"Jesus Christ, Mohammed, Jehovah, Allah. These are all names employed to describe an entity that is distinctly the same across the world."
—POPE FRANCIS?

At the beginning of 2017 some people were fooled into thinking Pope Francis was a relativist who condemned the idea of "segregating" different faiths. But Vatican spokesperson Greg Burke says this quote was "invented" by someone else.[59] An online search revealed the "inventor" to be an anonymous author from a website known for sharing "fake news" stories.[60]

Even the Atheists?

The Church teaches that a person is capable of choosing to do what is right even if he does not believe in God. That's because everyone, including atheists, has an innate knowledge of God's laws. According to St. Paul, "What the law requires is written on their hearts, while their conscience also bears witness and their conflicting thoughts accuse or perhaps excuse them on that day when, according to my gospel, God judges the secrets of men by Christ Jesus" (Rom. 2:15-16).

But this does not mean that God is outdated, that nature can be a church, or that our own actions make us "good enough" to earn our admittance into heaven as this apocryphal Pope Francis quote alleges. The true origin of the quote is probably someone misremembering a 2013 homily in which the pope addressed the possibility of salvation for atheists (the misquote started circulating in 2014). The part of the pope's homily that dealt with God's universal redemption of mankind was widely reprinted in news articles bearing headlines like "Pope Says Atheists Can Go to Heaven." Pope Francis said:

The Lord has redeemed all of us, all of us, with the Blood of Christ: all of us, not just Catholics. Everyone! "Father, the atheists?" Even the atheists. Everyone! And this Blood makes us children of God of the first class. We are created children in the likeness of God and the Blood of Christ has redeemed us all. And we all have a duty to do good. And this commandment for everyone to do good, I think, is a beautiful path toward peace.[61]

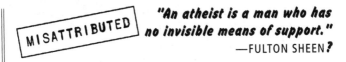

"An atheist is a man who has no invisible means of support."
—FULTON SHEEN ?

Most sources attribute the quote to the December 14, 1955 issue of *Look* magazine, but that issue does not exist. Fulton Sheen was featured in *Look*'s December 14, 1954 issue but it is currently out of print so I cannot confirm if it records Sheen speaking about atheists.[63] But the Protestant pastor Harry Emerson Fosdick wrote in 1943, "When, therefore, religious faith collapses, as it has in multitudes today, the nervous results are unmistakable. An atheist, says John Buchan [who served as Canada's governor general decades earlier], is 'a man who has no invisible means of support.'"[64]

This casts doubt on the claim that Fulton Sheen originally said this, but the quote's true source remains as invisible as the support atheists do not possess.

Fr. Thomas Rosica, a Canadian priest who serves as a media attaché for the Vatican, published a response to counter the media's oversimplification of the pope's remarks. He pointed out that Pope Francis is "first and foremost a seasoned pastor and preacher who has much experience in reaching people. His words are not spoken in the context of a theological faculty or academy nor in interreligious dialogue or debate."[62] In other words, Pope Francis's remarks were not a formal address about the Church's position on the salvation of non-Catholics. Instead, the pope was speaking about the general theme of God's universal love and redemption of mankind.

In that respect, Pope Francis was reiterating what the Church has always taught: Because God desires the salvation of all people (1 Tim. 2:4), salvation is possible for anyone. When Pope Francis said, "The Lord has redeemed all of us . . . Even the atheists," he was not deviating from Catholic doctrine. St. John said that Christ "is the expiation for our sins, and not for ours only but also for the sins of the whole world" (1 John 2:2). Consider also this excerpt from a Lenten sermon Pope Leo the Great gave in the fifth century:

> No one, however weak, is denied a share in the victory of the cross. No one is beyond the help of the prayer of Christ. His prayer brought benefit to the multitude that raged against him. How much more does it bring to those who turn to him in repentance. Ignorance has been destroyed, obstinacy has been overcome. The sacred blood of Christ has quenched the flaming sword that barred access to the tree of life. The age-old night of sin has given place to the true light.[65]

What does it mean to say everyone, including atheists, are *redeemed*? Redemption means "buying back" or "acquiring something from someone else." For example, we might say a performance in a film was the film's *redeeming* feature. That means the performance was so good that it outweighed the film's other negative features and single-handedly rescued the film from being bad and made it good.

In the context of Christianity, Christ's act of redeeming humanity means his death on the cross was so good that it outweighed the badness of our sins and the punishment they deserve. Because Christ is fully man, his death had value for human beings; and because Christ is God, his death had *infinite* value, meaning that it was more than sufficient to make up for humanity's sins.

"Every man who knocks at the door of a brothel is actually looking for God."
—G.K. CHESTERTON?

This is not found in any of Chesterton's extant works, but it can be found in Bruce Marshall's 1945 book *The World, The Flesh, and Father Smith.* In one passage, the book's titular character is having a conversation with a flirtatious young woman who chides him for his celibacy. She claims religion is just a substitute for sex, to which Fr. Smith responds, "I still prefer to believe that sex is a substitute for religion and that the young man who rings the bell at the brothel is unconsciously looking for God."[67]

Since Chesterton also wrote fictional stories involving a priest, the Father Brown series, it's possible that someone who read Marshall's work confused the two characters.

Christ's sacrifice also showed in a visceral way the depths of God's love for us. As St. Francis de Sales said: "In our Lord's passion love and death blend so inextricably that no heart can contain one without the other."[66] Through Christ's death on the cross all people have been redeemed, but not everyone is assured of heaven. That's because the process of salvation includes more than just redemption.

Christ's payment for the penalty of sin must be *applied* to each person's soul in order to unite him to God for all eternity. Some people may reject what Christ has done for them and not want to be freed from their particular sins. But others will accept God's grace and desire salvation from sin and eternal death. Salvation comes to these people through baptism, which cleanses them of sin and makes them adopted children of God. According to *The Catechism of the Catholic Church* (CCC), "all men may attain salvation through faith, Baptism and the observance of the Commandments" (2068).

Refuting Relativism

If God wants all people to be saved, then how can people who are never baptized be saved? A relativist would say that all people go to heaven and there is no such thing as one "true religion." A popular fake quote attributed to Pope Francis encapsulates this attitude: "All religions are true, because they are true in the hearts of all those who believe in them. What other kind of truth is there?"

According to Fr. Rosica, "Catholics do not adopt the attitude of religious relativism which regards all religions as on the whole equally justifiable, and the confusion and disorder among them as relatively unimportant."[68] In his first meeting with world leaders, Pope Francis rebuked modern relativism saying:

> There is another form of poverty! It is the spiritual poverty of our time, which afflicts the so-called richer countries particularly seriously. It is what my much-loved predecessor, Benedict XVI, called the "tyranny of relativism," which makes everyone his own criterion and endangers the coexistence of peoples. And that brings me to a second reason for my name. Francis of Assisi tells us we should work to build peace. But there is no true peace without truth![69]

According to the Second Vatican Council's declaration on the relation of the Church to non-Christian religions, "other religions found everywhere try to counter the restlessness of the human heart, each in its own manner, by proposing 'ways,' comprising teachings, rules of life, and sacred rites. The Catholic Church rejects nothing that is true and holy in these religions."[70]

For example, Muslims are correct that there is only one God and he is infinite in being, but they are incorrect when they deny that Jesus is the only begotten Son of God. Different religions have discovered various truths about God and Christ, but the fullness of God's revelation is found in the Church Jesus founded on Peter and the other apostles, the Catholic Church.

MISATTRIBUTED

"Fairy tales are more than true; not because they tell us dragons exist, but because they tell us dragons can be beaten."
—G.K. CHESTERTON?

Speaking of truth, this statement appears as an epigraph, or introductory quotation, attributed to Chesterton in the 2002 children's novella, *Coraline*. In 2013, Neil Gaiman, the author of *Coraline*, explained that this was a paraphrase of a passage he read in Chesterton's work *Tremendous Trifles*.[71]

In that work, Chesterton said that fairy tales do not create children's fears or "bogeymen." Instead, a fairy tale "accustoms [the child] for a series of clear pictures to the idea that these limitless terrors had a limit, that these shapeless enemies have enemies in the knights of God . . . Fairy tales do not give the child his first idea of bogey. What fairy tales give the child is his first clear idea of the possible defeat of bogey."[72]

Erroneous Exclusivism

While the relativist thinks every non-Catholic will be saved, the radical exclusivist claims the opposite—it is impossible for any non-Catholic to be saved. This belief is also called Feenyism after the late Jesuit priest Fr. Leonard Feeney.[73] His followers often defended their view by pointing to magisterial documents that contain the Latin phrase *Extra ecclesiam nulla salus*, or "Outside the Church there is no salvation." For example, a decree at the ecumenical Fourth Lateran Council said, "There is one Universal Church of the faithful, outside of which there is absolutely no salvation."[74]

According to the *Catechism*, "there is no salvation outside of the Church" means, "all salvation comes from Christ the Head through the Church, which is his Body" (846). Salvation does not come from purely human religious figures like Buddha or Muhammad. Neither does it come from purely human works of charity. Jesus told us no one can come to the Father except through him (John 14:6), and St. Peter said of Jesus, "There is salvation in no one else, for there is no other name under heaven given among men by which we must be saved" (Acts 4:12).

But acknowledging that Christ is the only objective way we are saved, or that only Christ takes away the sins of the world, does not mean that a person cannot be saved if he does not know this truth about Christ. For example, one could say that antivenom is the only way to be saved from a snakebite, but a child receiving antivenom does not have to know this truth in order to be saved from the bite. Similarly, a person could seek "the way" or "the truth" and strive to act with perfect charity without realizing that he was seeking after Christ, who, unbeknownst to him, is "the way, and the truth, and the life" (John 14:6).

"There is no saint without a past and no sinner without a future."
—ST. AUGUSTINE?

Early citations of this quote attribute it not to the wisdom of St. Augustine but to a general proverb that was common in India. One citation is Mirza Ahmad Sohrab's *A Persian Rosary of Nineteen Pearls* (1939) and the oldest reference I have located is a 1936 government report from the State of Vermont that says, "We do not expect perfection and there are always failures . . . We believe with the Persians, that—"There is no saint without a past and no sinner without a future."[75]

The Second Vatican Council considered the salvation of those who never heard the Gospel and as a result, were not baptized. For example, prior to the time of Columbus, Native Americans had no opportunity to believe in Christ or to be baptized.[76] Could they still be saved? Here's what the council said:

> Those also can attain to salvation who through no fault of their own do not know the gospel of Christ or his Church, yet sincerely seek God and moved by grace strive by their deeds to do his will as it is known to them through the dictates of conscience. Nor does divine Providence deny the helps necessary for salvation to those who, without blame on their part, have not yet arrived at an explicit knowledge of God and with his grace strive to live a good life.[77]

The *Catechism* also teaches that some people who lack faith, such as atheists, should not be held culpable for their nonbelief, because "believers can have more than a little to do with the rise of atheism. To the extent that they are careless about their instruction in the faith, or present its teaching falsely, or even fail in their religious, moral, or social life, they must be said to conceal rather than to reveal the true nature of God and of religion" (2125).

**"If there were no God,
there would be no atheists."**
—G.K. CHESTERTON?

Chesterton actually said: "If there were *not* God, there would be no atheists."[78] This isn't the pedantic observation that if God did not exist then atheists would not exist. Chesterton was pointing out that if God were not such an important part of the human experience, then no one would waste time debunking him. Chesterton writes in the same work that atheism lives in "an atmosphere of defiance and not of denial. Irreverence is a very servile parasite of reverence."[79]

But if anyone, including an atheist, can be saved, then why bother telling that person about the Faith at all? Don't we risk the person's soul by giving him an opportunity to reject the gospel? We do not, as can be seen through the following analogy:

Imagine you are trying to help people cross a river that has partially frozen over. The river is shrouded in fog, and when people choose to walk across its icy surface they disappear into the mist. Did they make it across? It's possible they safely made it, but it's also possible, if not probable, that many of them did not make it. Let's say, however, that you knew about a bridge that safely crosses over the river. Even if they might reject your offer, wouldn't you still tell people about this safer and more certain way to get across the river?[80]

Preaching the gospel doesn't endanger souls, because every person who never knew Jesus will not automatically go to heaven. Such people, like everyone else, are tempted by sin, and without God's grace it is even harder for these people to resist the devil's lies. The Church is, therefore, mindful of these people, and so it "fosters the missions with care and attention."[81] That's why Jesus commanded his followers to "make disciples of all nations, baptizing them in the name of the Father and of the Son and of the Holy Spirit" (Matt. 28:19).

A Better Quote

> *"God has bound salvation to the sacrament of Baptism, but he himself is not bound by his sacraments."*
> —*CATECHISM OF THE CATHOLIC CHURCH* 1257

Salvation from sin only comes from Jesus Christ, but this does not mean salvation is impossible for those who do not know the person of Jesus Christ or his Church. The *Catechism* tells us, "Baptism is necessary for salvation for those to whom the Gospel has been proclaimed and who have had the possibility of asking for this sacrament," (1257). Since God is all-powerful he can give saving grace to anyone at any time. This includes people who, through no fault of their own, never believed in him before death or never had the opportunity to be baptized.

4. "Pray as though everything depended on God, act as if everything depended on you."

—ST. IGNATIUS OF LOYOLA?

MOST PEOPLE THINK St. Ignatius of Loyola was a former soldier who forsook his irreligious ways after he found Christ while recovering from a combat wound in the hospital. He later founded the Society of Jesus, or the Jesuits, who have been called "God's Marines" by both supporters and critics in honor of their founder's military background. But like many stories about the saints, this one is not entirely accurate.

It's true Ignatius did not exemplify saintly behavior before his debilitating injury at the battle of Pamplona, but he did try to live out his faith and was not an irreligious derelict. He even wrote poems honoring St. Peter and the Blessed Virgin Mary.[82] St. Ignatius also was not a professional soldier. As a member of the upper class he received training in martial arts like sword fighting, but according to Jesuit scholar Fr. Barton Geger, "Ignatius never enlisted in an army, probably never fought in other battles besides Pamplona, and probably had little knowledge of military strategy."[83]

Fr. Geger is careful to note, however, that some people dramatically *understate* Ignatius's military experience, which is also incorrect. St. Ignatius often wore armor, carried weapons in public, and was not hesitant to use them. On one occasion he tried to duel with a Moor who denied Mary's perpetual virginity but was providentially guided away from the town where the Moor had gone.[84] The Jesuit's founding document is addressed to "Whoever desires to serve as a soldier of God beneath the banner of the cross in our Society."[85]

The imagery of a soldier resolutely marching into battle may also have given rise to this famous quote attributed to Ignatius (and sometimes St. Augustine): "Pray as though everything depended on God, act as if everything depended on you."

> MISATTRIBUTED
>
> **"Lord, grant me the strength to change the things I can, the serenity to deal with the things I cannot change, and the wisdom to know the difference."**
> —ST. FRANCIS OF ASSISI?
>
> The Protestant theologian Reinhold Niebuhr wrote what is now commonly called the "Serenity Prayer." The earliest version of the prayer comes from a 1927 Christian student newsletter that attributes this prayer to Niebuhr: "Father, give us courage to change what must be altered, serenity to accept what cannot be helped, and the insight to know the one from the other."[86] The prayer increased in popularity after a secretary at Alcoholics Anonymous noticed it in a 1941 *New York Herald Tribune* obituary.[87]

Everything Depends on Me?

Some people think this quote is authentic because paragraph 2834 of the *Catechism* attributes it to Ignatius.[88] But the *Catechism* is not inerrant like Sacred Scripture. Some of the teachings described in the *Catechism* are infallible, but according to Cardinals Schönborn and Ratzinger, "the individual doctrine which the *Catechism* presents receive no other weight than that which they already possess."[89]

This means that the *Catechism* is a collection of both unchanging, infallible dogmas and teachings that have not been infallibly defined. The *Catechism* also includes prudential judgments on topics like the application of the death penalty, about which Cardinal Ratzinger says, "There may be a legitimate diversity of opinion even among Catholics."[90] Even in the sections of the *Catechism* that describe infallible dogmas, the gift of infallibility only extends to divinely revealed matters of faith and morals. It does not ensure that scientific or historical facts, including citations for quotations that support those dogmas or doctrines, are without error.

Regarding the quote in paragraph 2834, the *Catechism* cites Joseph Guibert's nineteenth-century study of the Jesuits. But in a footnote on the page the *Catechism* cites, the editor of Guibert's book (which was published after his death) says of the popular Ignatian quote, "In this precise formula, the thought is nowhere found in Ignatius' writings nor in any contemporary documents; but nevertheless it does correspond to his ideas."[91] The closest parallel is found in Pedro de Ribadeneira's biography of Ignatius, which was written less than twenty years after Ignatius' death. He writes:

> In matters which he took up pertaining to the service of our Lord, he made use of all the human means to succeed in them, with a care and efficiency as great as if the success depended on these means; and he confided in God and depended on his providence as greatly as if all the other human means which he was using were of no effect.[92]

PROBABLY FAKE

"Start by doing what's necessary; then do what's possible; and suddenly you are doing the impossible."
—ST. FRANCIS OF ASSISI?

Despite its popularity on the Internet, I have not located a source written before 1993 that records St. Francis saying what sounds like a slogan from a motivational speaking workshop. In fact, one researcher says this only sounds like St. Francis "if your idea of St. Francis is a 13th-century Zig Ziglar. In other words, it fails the 'sounds right' test."[93] A better piece of advice comes from St. Josemaría Escrivá who said, "With God's grace, you have to tackle and carry out the impossible, because anybody can do what is possible."[94]

The earliest citation of this quote I have found comes from an 1868 edition of the *American Phrenological Journal*, which attributes the following variant to St. Ignatius: "Pray as if everything depended on prayer; then work as if everything depended on work."[95] But one year earlier an Evangelical journal cited John Wesley, the founder of Methodism, as saying, "Work and preach as if everything depended on you, but pray as if everything depended on God."[96] Other late-nineteenth-century and early-twentieth-century works call the maxim "an old saying" and don't attribute it to anyone. This casts doubt on the idea that the quote has been known as a piece of the wisdom of St. Ignatius of Loyola since the sixteenth century.

In response, some people claim this quote is a mistranslation of the following authentic Ignatian saying, "Let your first rule of action be to trust in God as if success depended entirely on yourself and not on him: but use all your efforts as if God alone did everything, and yourself nothing." In other words, what St. Ignatius really said was, "Pray as though everything depended on you, and act as if everything depended on God."

Although this is closer in tone to other paradoxical elements in Ignatius's writings, the earliest appearance of this saying is in a collection of Ignatian wisdom that was written 150 years after his death.[97] It is more likely to be authentic than the previous quote but we are still far from certain that it actually comes from St. Ignatius of Loyola.

Praying It Will Work Out

Even if both these quotations are apocryphal, don't they still teach a valuable lesson? They can if they are properly understood.

For example, telling someone to act as if everything depended on them can reduce the temptation never to take any initiative and simply "leave things up to God." In the seventeenth century, the Quietist heresy taught that mankind's ultimate goal was to achieve "perfect quiet" and be so united to God in prayer that one did not have a single thought in the mind. These people literally prayed as if everything depended on God and did nothing else. But saying we should work as if it *only* "depended on us" can reduce God's role in our lives to a mere afterthought in prayer. According to biblical scholar J.P.M. Walsh:

> The popular form of the maxim is also congenial to certain instincts in us: to focus on our own efforts, to act as if things are all up to us, to reduce God's working in our lives to a prepositional phrase: "with God's help." I play my part, and God plays his. Sometimes the maxim is used in such a way that it is virtually interchangeable with the bromide, "God helps those who help themselves."[98]

Christians can't separate prayer and work into watertight compartments that never overlap but only happen in successive order. Prayer is not the time to seek God's help before we "get the job done ourselves." In his encyclical on human work, Pope St. John Paul II wrote, "Let the Christian who listens to the word of the living God, uniting work with prayer, know the place that his work has not only in earthly progress but also in the development of the Kingdom of God, to which we are all called through the power of the Holy Spirit and through the word of the Gospel."[99]

Everything we do, including prayer, is only possible because of God's gracious assistance. St. Paul says, "The Spirit helps us in our weakness; for we do not know how to pray as we ought, but the Spirit himself intercedes for us with sighs too deep for words" (Rom. 8:26). In a letter he wrote to Francis Borgia in 1555, St. Ignatius provides a sound perspective on the relationship between human efforts and divine providence:

> I consider it an error to trust and hope in any means or efforts in themselves alone; nor do I consider it a safe path to trust the whole matter to God our Lord without desiring to help myself by what he has given me; so that it seems to me in our Lord that I ought to make use of both parts, desiring in all things his greater praise and glory, and nothing else.[100]

The Prayer of St. Francis

Now that we've addressed the "me-centered" spirituality that can come from this previous apocryphal Ignatius quote, we can address two other quotes that reinforce this attitude. You've probably heard the first if you attend liturgies that prefer to use contemporary music sung under the title "The Prayer of St. Francis" or "Prayer for Peace." Here's an excerpt to refresh your memory:

Lord, make me an instrument of your peace.
Where there is hatred, let me bring love . . .

O Master, let me not seek as much
to be consoled as to console . . .

. . . it is in pardoning that one is pardoned,
it is in dying that one is raised to eternal life.

Contrary to the prayer's title, it first appeared in a 1912
issue of the French Catholic devotional magazine *La Clo-
chette*, where it was simply called *"Belle prière à faire pendant la
messe"* ("A beautiful prayer to say during the Mass"). Augustine Thompson notes in his biography of St. Francis, "Noble
as its sentiments are, Francis would not have written such a
piece, focused as it is on the self, with its constant repetition
of the pronouns 'I' and 'me,' the words 'God' and 'Jesus' never
appearing once."[101]

Christian Renoux, who authored a book-length study of
the Prayer of St. Francis, says the pieces in this magazine were
anonymous but may have been written by the magazine's editor, Fr. Esther Bouquerel. It is not known, however, if Fr.
Bouquerel wrote what would later become known as "The
Prayer of St. Francis."

The prayer's identification with St. Francis probably occurred in 1918, after a Franciscan priest named Father Étienne
Benoît printed it on a holy card whose reverse side contained
an image of his order's founder. Fr. Benoît did not attribute
the prayer to St. Francis and only included the title *Prière pour
la paix*, or "Prayer for peace." According to Renoux:

The first translation in English that we know of appeared
in 1936 in *Living Courageously*, a book by Kirby Page (1890-
1957), a Disciple of Christ minister, pacifist, social evan-

gelist, writer and editor of *The World Tomorrow* . . . Page clearly attributed the text to St. Francis of Assisi. During World War II and immediately after, this prayer for peace began circulating widely as the Prayer of St. Francis.[102]

In 1967, Sebastian Temple, himself a third-order Dominican, set the prayer to music in a song now known as "The Prayer of St. Francis" or "Make Me a Channel of Your Peace." However, if you desire to say a prayer that more closely corresponds to the thought of St. Francis, then I recommend this one from his disciple St. Giles:

Blessed is he who loves and does not
therefore desire to be loved.

Blessed is he who fears and does not
therefore desire to be feared.

Blessed is he who serves and does not
therefore desire to be served.

Blessed is he who behaves well toward
others and does not desire that others
behave well toward him.

And because these are great things, the
foolish do not rise to them.[103]

"If you are what you should be, you will set the whole world ablaze!"
—ST. CATHERINE OF SIENA **?**

In a letter to Fr. Dom Stefano Marconi, who served as one of Catherine's scribes, she wrote, "If you are what you ought to be, you will set fire to all Italy, and not only yonder."[104] The misquote gained popularity after Pope St. John Paul II used it in his homily at the closing mass for the 2000 World Youth Day in Toronto, though both quotes share a similar meaning.

Christ Has No Body?

One particularly egregious example of "me-centered spirituality" can be seen in this poem that is attributed to the sixteenth-century Carmelite nun St. Teresa of Avila. It's usually called "Christ Has No Body":

> Christ has no body now but yours. No hands, no feet on earth but yours. Yours are the eyes through which he looks compassion on this world. Yours are the feet with which he walks to do good. Yours are the hands through which he blesses all the world. Yours are the hands, yours are the feet, yours are the eyes, you are his body. Christ has no body now on earth but yours.

The poem's theology alone should make us skeptical that it came from St. Teresa because it is very misleading, if not false, to say "Christ has no body now on earth but yours." The Eucharist is the body of Christ (CCC 1375) and the mystical body of Christ exists on earth through the spiritual union of living believers (CCC 788, Rom. 12:5). It's true that Christ no longer dwells on earth in a human body, but that is not the same as saying, "Christ has no body now but yours."

This poem is also not found in St. Teresa's writings or in any early biographies written about her. According to researcher Timothy Phillips, the true origin of this quote lies in two nineteenth-century Protestant writers.[105] The second half of the quote can be found in this portion of an 1888 sermon by Methodist minister Mark Guy Pearse:

> Now you, my brothers and sisters, are the eyes through which Christ's compassion is to look out upon this world, and yours are the lips through which his love is to speak; yours are the hands with which he is to bless men, and yours the feet with which he is to go about doing good— through his Church, which is his body.[106]

Four years later, a Quaker medical missionary named Sarah Eliza Rowntree cited Pearse's sermon and added what has now become the first part of the apocryphal Teresa quote. She said, "Remember Christ has no human body now upon the earth but yours; no hands but yours; no feet but yours."[107]

There is nothing wrong with exhorting people to represent Christ on earth and to figuratively be his "hands and feet." St. Paul told the Corinthians to "be imitators of me, as I am of Christ" (1 Cor. 11:1), and he told the Galatians, "I have been crucified with Christ; it is no longer I who live, but Christ who lives in me" (Gal. 2:20). We can be Christ for others without causing confusion about how Christ is present on earth today.

St. Teresa offered this advice, which is helpful to anyone who desires to "be Christ" for others: "Think not of the faults of others but of their virtues and of your own faults . . . Always think of yourself as everyone's servant; look for Christ Our Lord in everyone and you will then have respect and reverence for all."[108]

A Better Quote

> ### *"Apart from me you can do nothing."*
> (JOHN 15:5)

Jesus never said that God's will is accomplished only after we add our purely human efforts to his divine efforts. Instead, Christ tells us that we are connected to him like branches are connected to a vine, and so all the good we do is only possible because of that connection. He tells the disciples, "I am the vine, you are the branches. He who abides in me, and I in him, he it is that bears much fruit, for apart from me you can do nothing" (John 15:5).

5. "God helps those who help themselves."

DURING HIS TENURE as the host of *The Tonight Show*, Jay Leno would approach random people on the street and ask them basic questions about American history or culture—questions they usually bungled. The hapless subjects of these "Jay-walking" segments didn't fare any better when asked about religion.

Some memorable answers include Jesus being born 250 million years ago, Richard Nixon finding the burning bush, and Joe DiMaggio being swallowed by a whale.[109] A fair number of the respondents also thought that one of the Ten Commandments was "God helps those who help themselves." According to researcher George Barna, "The most quoted 'Bible verse' in America is: 'God helps those who help themselves'; 82 percent believe that is a direct quote from the Bible."[110]

The irony, of course, is that America's most memorable Bible verse is not only not in the Bible, it undermines what the Bible does say.

Hercules Helps Those Who Help Themselves

The idea that "God helps those who help themselves" has its roots in ancient Greek drama. In Euripides' play *Hippolytus*, a character says, "Try first thyself, and after call in God;/For to the worker God himself lends aid."[111] The similar idea, "God *doesn't* help those who *don't* help themselves," can be seen in the writings of Sophocles, who says in his play *Philocetes*, "Heaven helps not the men who will not act."[112] The most famous portrayal of this idea is the story of *Hercules and the Wagoner,* which was later included in collections of Aesop's fables.

In that story, a man pulling a wagon becomes stuck in a ravine or patch of mud. He cries out for the divine strongman Hercules to assist him. Hercules then appears and says, "Put your shoulder to the wheel, man, and goad on your horses, and then you may call on Hercules to assist you. If you won't lift a finger to help yourself, you can't expect Hercules or anyone else to come to your aid." The fable ends with this piece of advice: "Heaven helps those who help themselves."[113]

"Spare the rod, spoil the child."
—THE BIBLE?

This appears to be a paraphrase of Proverbs 13:24, "He who spares the rod hates his son, but he who loves him is diligent to discipline him." The emphasis of the verse is on loving a child by providing him the discipline he needs. Although the use of corporal punishment was common in the ancient world (and still is in many places today), the truth of this passage is not diminished if a parent chooses to use noncorporal forms of discipline.

In the sixteenth and seventeenth centuries, European authors collected the writings of ancient fabulists like Aesop in order to compose their own collections of didactic short stories. One of the most famous was the *Fables* of Jean de la Fontaine, which includes the tale of "The Mired Carter" and Fontaine's summary of its moral: *"Aide-toi, le ciel t'aidera,"* or "Help yourself and Heaven will help you too." At around the same time, the English political theorist Algernon Sidney wrote *Discourses Concerning Government,* which gave us the proverb as we know it today.

Sidney was a vociferous opponent of the absolute monarchy, or the idea that most if not all political authority was found in a single king or royal figure. He argued instead that God desired human beings to set up their own forms of government as they saw fit. In one section of the book he says that a man cannot expect the State alone to protect him just as the State does not expect God alone to protect it. Instead, the State makes use of the resources God has given it and individual men must be prepared to do the same. Hence, Algernon writes,

> God helps those who help themselves; and men are by several reasons (suppose to prevent the increase of a suspected power) induced to succour an industrious and brave people: But such as neglect the means of their own preservation, are ever left to perish with shame.[114]

The book's arguments became very popular among leaders of the American Revolution, who rejected the authority of the British crown and wanted a more representative form of government. One of them was Benjamin Franklin, who included the proverb in an almanac he wrote under the pseudonym "Poor Richard." *Poor Richard's Almanac* also included valuable weather forecasts and entertaining puzzles, which made it a best-selling book among the American colonists. Sidney's proverb is found among others that are still recited today, like "Fish and visitors stink after three days," or "Hunger is the best pickle."

Poor Richard's wisdom was probably conflated with Scripture because of a "Protestant work ethic" that was common among the colonists and still persists in many parts of America today. Barna says, "[This proverb] perfectly summarizes American theology. In essence, it teaches that we must make things happen on the strength of our own abilities and efforts, and when we prove ourselves capable of succeeding in achieving our goals, then God is obligated to bless us."[115]

The Bible on God's Help

The Bible praises the value of hard work, as can be seen in Proverbs 13:4, which says, "The soul of the sluggard craves, and gets nothing, while the soul of the diligent is richly supplied." Proverbs also gives this advice: "Commit your work to the Lord, and your plans will be established" (16:3). In one sense, God does help those who do good for others or even themselves. But it is not true that God's help is reserved for those "who help themselves." In fact, Scripture teaches that God has a special concern for those who cannot help themselves.

Psalm 68:5 describes God as the "Father of the fatherless and protector of widows." In the ancient world, those who lacked parents or a spouse risked enslavement or starvation, so they needed someone else to help them out of their dire circumstances. That's why James 1:17 says, "Religion that is pure and undefiled before God and the Father is this: to visit orphans and widows in their affliction."

When the Blessed Virgin Mary praised God as her savior, she didn't boast about her own accomplishments that spurred God to intervene on her behalf. Instead, she thanked God because he "regarded the low estate of his handmaiden," and it was for this reason all generations would call her blessed (Luke 1:47-48). Mary said of those who were great at helping themselves, like the proud, the mighty, and the filled, that God would scatter, put down, and send them away empty (Luke 1:51-53). She then said that God "has helped his servant Israel, in remembrance of his mercy"—not because of anything Israel did itself.

Scripture even warns against trusting one's efforts apart from God, or as Proverbs 28:25-26 says, "A greedy man stirs up strife, but he who trusts in the Lord will be enriched. He who trusts in his own mind is a fool; but he who walks in wisdom will be delivered." This becomes all the more obvious when we examine God's help in the matter of sin and how he delivers us from eternal damnation.

"God moves in mysterious ways"
—THE BIBLE?

The origin of this phrase may be an eighteenth-century hymn written by William Cowper, which says, in part, "God moves in a mysterious way/His wonders to perform/He plants his footsteps in the sea/And rides upon the storm."[116] Although this hymn is not in Scripture, the mystery of God's plans is described in Isaiah 55:8-9, where the prophet says, "For my thoughts are not your thoughts, neither are your ways my ways, says the Lord. For as the heavens are higher than the earth, so are my ways higher than your ways and my thoughts than your thoughts."

A Spiritual Stairway to Heaven

Once when I was browsing the Internet I saw a picture of someone walking on the beach. Alongside were these words: "To fall in love with God is the greatest of all romances; to seek him, the greatest adventure; to find him, the greatest human achievement." The quote was attributed to St. Augustine, but it actually comes from Fr. Raphael Simon, and appeared in his 1961 book *The Glory of Thy People: The Story of a Conversion*.[117] In fact, Augustine had to refute a heresy called Pelagianism, which turned man's relationship with God into a human achievement.

Pelagius, from whom the heresy gets its name, was born in the British Isles in A.D. 360. Twenty years later he came to the city of Rome as a respected monk and spiritual director. However, he became distraught at the moral laxity among some of the people. Pelagius blamed this on Augustine's teaching that grace was necessary to overcome sin, which he thought allowed people to blame God's lack of grace for their sins. In response, he taught that man could, by his own ability, overcome the effects of original sin and keep God's law through discipline apart from grace.

"This too shall pass."
—THE BIBLE **?**

St. Teresa of Avila did say, "All things are passing; God never changes," but it is not a biblical verse.[118] A similar thought can be found in Paul's second letter to the Corinthians, in which he re-assures his audience that they are "treasures in earthen vessels" that are being renewed daily by faith in the risen Jesus. Even if they are afflicted, it will be compensated by a future resurrection to glory. He writes:

> For this slight momentary affliction is preparing for us an eternal weight of glory beyond all comparison, because we look not to the things that are seen but to the things that are unseen; for the things that are seen are transient, but the things that are unseen are eternal (2 Cor. 4:17-18).

Pelagius's teachings were condemned at the Council of Carthage in A.D. 418, and he disappeared from the historical record shortly after that time. But heresies are like the hydra of Greek mythology: as soon as you cut off one head two more grow back in its place. In this case, Augustine's refutations of Pelagianism led to the development of a similar heresy we now call semi-Pelagianism.

Semi-Pelagians agreed with Augustine that a person could not obey God's law and remain free from sin apart from the gift of God's grace. Where they disagreed with Augustine was on the question of how someone received God's grace in the first place. Semi-Pelagians taught that a person in a state of original sin could, on his own initiative, approach God and seek his offer of salvation. While a person could not *grow* in his faith apart from grace, he could *begin* his journey of faith apart from God's grace. In other words, "God helps those [to attain his saving grace], who help themselves [toward that saving grace]."

Semi-Pelagianism was condemned at the Council of Orange in A.D. 529 because it contradicts the Bible's teaching that our salvation neither increases nor even begins apart from the grace of God. At every point in our salvation God's grace is present to deliver us from sin and death. Ephesians 2:8-9 says, "For by grace you have been saved through faith; and this is not your own doing, it is the gift of God—not because of works, lest any man should boast."

Contrary to what some Protestants teach, however, this does not mean human beings lack free will or that our choices play no part in our salvation. God predestines no one to spend eternity in hell (CCC 1037), and he gives everyone an opportunity to receive his saving grace. No one can freely choose to come to God apart from his grace, but anyone can freely choose to reject God in spite of that grace. This exemplifies Jesus' declaration that "many are called, but few are chosen" (Matt. 22:14).

God's Ultimate Help

The *Catechism* teaches: "Since the initiative belongs to God in the order of grace, no one can merit the initial grace of forgiveness and justification, at the beginning of conversion" (2010). The Council of Trent likewise declared: "None of those things which precede justification—whether faith or works—merit the grace itself of justification. For, if it be a grace, it is not now by works, otherwise, as the same Apostle says, grace is no more grace [Rom. 11:6]."[119]

Nothing we do, be it a good work or even an act of faith, causes God to give us his grace. God's offer of salvation is instead a free gift we accept or reject. Some Protestants might say we accept this gift by faith and only faith is required for salvation, but that is not what the Bible teaches. According to James 2:24, "A man is justified by works and not by faith alone." Paul said we must "work out our salvation" (Phil. 2:12) in the present because we are in the process of "being saved" (1 Cor. 15:2).

God does not control every aspect of our lives (since we must work out our salvation) nor does he sit back and watch us vainly struggle to reach him through our own efforts (since God is saving us in this very moment). Instead, God gives us grace that allows us to enter into a saving relationship with him, but he does not give his grace only or primarily to those who have "helped themselves." One of Jesus' parables even shows that this gift of justification, or being made right in God's eyes, is especially for those who are so weighed down by sin that they cannot "help themselves."

In Luke 18, Jesus described two men praying at the Temple. One was a devout Pharisee who boasted of his good works but failed to confess any of his sins. The other was a lowly tax collector who couldn't even bear to look at heaven because he knew he was a sinner who had exploited his fellow Jews. Instead of boasting about his works, the tax collector merely said, "God, be merciful to me a sinner" (Luke 18:13). Jesus then told the crowd, "This man went down to his house justified rather than the other; for everyone who exalts himself will be humbled, but he who humbles himself will be exalted" (Luke 18:14).

The point of this parable is not, as some Protestants allege, that works do not contribute to our salvation. The Calvinist theologian Richard Gaffin, Jr., says there was nothing wrong with the Pharisee thanking God for helping him to do good deeds. But, "what is wrong and deeply flawed is what is missing (and present in the tax collector's prayer): a heartfelt confession of his own sinfulness and guilt."[120]

The Pharisee may have thought that God would help those who make an effort to be holy—that God helps believers who "help themselves." But Jesus taught that he loves even those who feel trapped in their sins and see no way out. The tax collector's humble, repentant prayer proves that God helps those who trust in him, regardless of how well they are able to "help themselves."

A Better Quote

"I can do all things in him who strengthens me."
(PHIL. 4:13)

God's help isn't a transactional exchange where we receive divine assistance after our human efforts have been exhausted. Instead, our human efforts are futile apart from God and so we should trust in God through everything we do by uniting our efforts with his grace.

In the fourth chapter of his letter to the Philippians, Paul thanked this church for their support during his personal hardships; but he reminded the Philippians that these hardships aren't insurmountable. He wrote, "I have learned, in whatever state I am, to be content. I know how to be abased, and I know how to abound; in any and all circumstances I have learned the secret of facing plenty and hunger, abundance and want" (Phil. 4:11-12).

What is the source of Paul's perpetual contentment? The answer is the Lord Jesus Christ. Paul says, "I can do all things in him who strengthens me" (Phil. 4:13).

PART II

Faith
and
Reason

6. "The truth is like a lion. You don't have to defend it. Let it loose. It will defend itself."

—ST. AUGUSTINE?

In 2017 Italian archbishop and president of the Pontifical Academy for Life Vincenzo Paglia told a reporter that Pope Francis's reform of the Academy "requires a redesign, a widening of perspectives, more areas of study, a renewal." The reporter asked Paglia, "Do you realize that, for many Catholics, what you say is considered as a reluctance to fight for Christian values?" Archbishop Paglia replied, "I am so certain of the power of Christian values that I don't feel a need to defend them, they defend themselves."[121]

With all due respect to the archbishop, it's not true that Christian values do not need us to defend them.[122] In the early Church, the value of grace had to be defended against the Pelagians, the value of Christ's divinity had to be defended against the Arians, and the value of human life had to be defended against the barbarians. In the modern world, the value of faith has to be defended against atheists, the value of the Church has to be defended against Protestants, and the value of unborn children has to be defended against advocates of abortion.

But those who claim that the truth "defends itself" sometimes enlist St. Augustine in support of their cause and claim the truth is a kind of wild animal that will devour error as long as we "let it loose."

Somebody's Lion About Augustine

When I first heard this quote I was immediately suspicious of its authenticity. It sounds more like a modern writer's attempt to come up with a clever saying than something from Augustine's writings. One clue that confirmed my suspicions is that the quote does not appear in any Internet searches of Augustine's works. Even a search of his entire body of writings in their original Latin text fails to produce any passages in which the words "lion" (*leo*) and "truth" (*veritas*) are found in close proximity to one another.[123]

Finally, I could not locate a single book attributing this saying to Augustine that was written before the twenty-first century. If Augustine had actually penned these words, then we would expect some writer to have quoted him between the fifth and twentieth centuries.

"The Catholic faith is like a lion in a cage. You don't need to defend it—you simply need to open the cage door."
—VENERABLE FULTON J. SHEEN**?**

Like Augustine's version, I was unable to find any citations for this quote and no references to it before 2006. It's possible that Archbishop Sheen uttered these words in one of his television programs, but in the absence of any direct evidence, I strongly suggest that this quote is as apocryphal as the version attributed to Augustine.

Although it may not be the origin of this quote, a strikingly similar passage can be found in the writings of Protestant pastor Charles Spurgeon. In one of his sermons he said, "Let the pure Gospel go forth in all its lion-like majesty and it will soon clear its own way and ease itself of its adversaries."[124] In an address he gave to the British and Foreign Bible Society, Spurgeon used a similar illustration, comparing the Bible to a magnificent lion. He said that while some would attack the lion and others rush to its defense, he thought it would be better to do this:

> Open the door and let the lion out; he will take care of himself. Why, they are gone! He no sooner goes forth in his strength than his assailants flee. The way to meet infidelity is to spread the Bible. The answer to every objection against the Bible is the Bible.[125]

How to Handle the Truth

Some people may believe Augustine thought the "truth is like a lion" because they believe another common saying: "The truth is its own defense." When these people hear that someone accused of a crime refuses to testify in court (or that he pleads the Fifth), they might say, "See, he has something to hide. Why doesn't he just get up there and tell the truth? After all, the truth needs no defense."

This kind of attitude gives defense attorneys ulcers. They know that even if their client is innocent, a skilled prosecutor can make them look guilty by asking complicated questions that result in the defendant giving inconsistent or suspicious answers. *Knowing* something is true is different than being able to *prove* it's true to a skeptical audience. Similarly, when a Christian presents the gospel to nonbelievers, he should also be prepared to answer objections to the truth he is presenting. In his first letter to the entire Church, St. Peter exhorted persecuted Christians to do just that:

> Even if you do suffer for righteousness' sake, you will be blessed. Have no fear of them, nor be troubled, but in your hearts reverence Christ as Lord. Always be prepared to make

a defense to any one who calls you to account for the hope that is in you, yet do it with gentleness and reverence; and keep your conscience clear, so that, when you are abused, those who revile your good behavior in Christ may be put to shame. (1 Pet. 3:14-16)

The Greek word St. Peter used to encourage Christians to "make a defense" is *apologian*. It refers to giving a reason or defense of an action, usually in the context of a court of law. Over five hundred years before the birth of Christ, the Greek philosopher Plato recorded his teacher Socrates' defense of himself before the rulers of Athens in a work called *Apology*. The modern word *apologetics* comes from *apologian* and refers not to apologizing for wrongdoing, but to presenting reasons and evidence in favor of a certain belief system.

"If you believe what you like in the gospels, and reject what you don't like, it is not the gospel you believe, but yourself."
—ST. AUGUSTINE**?**

Augustine did express this sentiment to the heretic Faustus, but with different words. He criticized Faustus for only recognizing the authority of the Gospel of John and not the other evangelists by saying, "For to believe what you please, and not to believe what you please, is to believe yourselves, and not the gospel."[126]

While there are apologists for a variety of religions, belief systems, and even certain sports teams, apologetics has traditionally been considered a branch of theology that provides the rational basis for the Christian faith. Instead of just letting the truth roam about like a lion, apologists "destroy arguments and every proud obstacle to the knowledge of God, and take every thought captive to obey Christ" (2 Cor. 10:5). The New Testament provides several examples of believers who used arguments and careful reasoning to defend the truth and refute error.

The critics who confronted Stephen, one of the Church's first deacons, "could not withstand the wisdom and the Spirit with which he spoke" (Acts 6:10). A believer named Apollos also "powerfully confuted the Jews in public, showing by the scriptures that the Christ was Jesus" (Acts 18:28). When St. Paul visited the Greek capital of Athens, he used the Athenian's natural religious behavior (or their worship of an "unknown god") to show how this God made himself known by raising Jesus Christ from the dead (Acts 17:22-31).

In the second century, Christians faced persecution from Jews who believed they had failed to keep the faith of their forefathers as well as from Romans who thought this new religion was a danger to the social order. Justin Martyr, who would later become the patron saint of apologists, answered both groups of critics. In his dialogue with Rabbi Trypho, Justin answered the charge that the disciples stole Jesus' body, and proved how Old Testament prophecies were fulfilled in the life of Christ. Justin also wrote to the Roman emperor and said that instead of being a threat to the social order, Christianity was essential to it:

> More than all other men are we your helpers and allies in promoting peace, seeing that we hold this view: that it is alike impossible for the wicked, the covetous, the conspirator, and for the virtuous, to escape the notice of God, and that each man goes to everlasting punishment or salvation according to the value of his actions.[127]

Even when Catholicism became the official religion of the Roman Empire, the responsibility of defending it did not disappear. This is evident in the writings of St. Augustine, who did not believe one must simply "let the Faith loose." For example, Augustine's *City of God* is a defense of Christian civilization and includes this description of how apologetics can become a means to evangelize those who attack the Faith:

> For while the hot restlessness of heretics stirs questions about many articles of the Catholic faith, the necessity of defending them forces us both to investigate them more accurately, to understand them more clearly, and to proclaim them more earnestly; and the question mooted by an adversary becomes the occasion of instruction.[128]

Aquinas Has Some Explaining to Do

Those who say the truth needs no defending are also apt to say the faith needs no explaining, or as St. Thomas Aquinas allegedly said, "To one who has faith, no explanation is necessary. To one without faith, no explanation is possible." In order to show why Thomas Aquinas did not say this, we must first examine his life and work.

At the age of nineteen, Thomas decided to join the newly founded Dominican order. This displeased his wealthy family so much that they imprisoned him in the family castle for over a year. After he escaped, Thomas enrolled at the University of Paris; but because of his wide girth and reluctance to speak some of his classmates called him "the dumb ox." This prompted one of the university's most distinguished professors, Albert Magnus, to declare, "You call him 'the Dumb Ox,' but one day the bellowing of this Ox will resound throughout the world."[129]

Thomas revitalized theology by applying recently rediscovered principles from Greek philosophy to the explanation and defense of the Christian faith. Thomas would never have said, "To one who has faith, no explanation is necessary," since he wrote an explanation of the Catholic faith for beginners called the *Summa Theologiae*. Likewise, he would not have said, "To one without faith, no explanation is possible," since his *Summa Contra Gentiles* was written to explain the Faith to non-Catholics like Muslims and Jews. The book's full title is *"Liber de veritate catholicae fidei contra errores infidelium,"* or "Book on the truth of the Catholic faith against the errors of the unbelievers."

"If the highest aim of a captain were to preserve his ship, he would keep it in port forever."
—ST. THOMAS AQUINAS*?*

At first I thought this was a misremembering of the late John A. Shedd's quotation: "A ship in harbor is safe, but that is not what ships are built for." But in the *Summa Theologiae* there is a refutation of the idea that man's happiness comes from merely preserving his bodily existence. Thomas says that a man's bodily existence is a means to his heavenly existence and not an end in itself. He then compares the idea of endlessly preserving the body with permanently keeping a ship in port: "A captain does not intend as a last end, the preservation of the ship entrusted to him, since a ship is ordained to something else as its end."[130]

The closest Thomas comes to saying the Faith needs no explanation is in the part of the *Summa Theologiae* that answers the question, "Can articles of faith be subjects of scientific inquiry?" In Thomas's time science was not restricted to naturalistic explanations of the universe; theology was even called "the queen of the sciences." Instead, science involved a systematic presentation of knowledge that resulted in demonstrable conclusions (the English word "science" comes from the Latin word *scientia*, which means knowledge).

Thomas then answers this argument: Articles of faith can be objects of scientific inquiry because scientific inquiry is only lacking in subjects where there is ignorance. Because we are not ignorant of the articles of faith, it follows that science is able to study these things and provide demonstrable conclusions about them from principles everyone observes. However, Thomas disagrees and says that articles of faith cannot be objects of scientific study. That's because science is derived from self-evident or "seen" principles, whereas articles of faith are sometimes derived from "unseen principles" that come from divine revelation. He writes:

> Unbelievers are in ignorance of things that are of faith, for neither do they see or know them in themselves, nor do they know them to be credible. The faithful, on the other hand, know them, not as by demonstration, but by the light of faith which makes them see that they ought to believe them.[131]

Note that this only applies to the foundational principles of the faith, and not to inferences and reasons that are drawn from these principles. So, for example, we know from divine revelation that God is a Trinity and this fact cannot be demonstrated from principles all people can naturally observe or "see." However, the logical reasoning that explains how there is no contradiction in one God existing as three persons is something that all people can investigate even if they disagree with the object of the reasoning, or in this case, the doctrine of the Trinity.

Thomas goes on to say that "holy men" prove the things of faith not by scientific demonstrations, but with "persuasive arguments showing that what is proposed to our faith is not impossible, or else they are proofs drawn from the principles of faith."[132] A person can and should explain the faith but he won't be able to do so entirely from natural principles. But the systematic explanations he can provide does mean theology, or the study of divine revelation, is a science. According to Thomas, "Whatever is based on these principles is as well proved in the eyes of the faithful, as a conclusion drawn from self-evident principles is in the eyes of all. Hence again, theology is a science, as we stated at the outset of this work."[133]

Unless Someone Teaches Me . . .

Those who say "the truth needs no defense" might also believe that because the Bible is God's truth it only needs to be preached and not defended. For example, after I finished a presentation on the Church's teaching on marriage and same-sex unions, a gentleman approached me and said, "Thank you so much for that presentation, but it wasn't what I expected."

"What were you expecting?" I asked.

"You gave a lot of good arguments and statistics, but I think you should have had more of the Bible in your presentation. After all, when God's word is sent out it never returns void."

I explained to this man that since the United States does not pass purely religious laws, it would be futile only to make a biblical case for marriage. My presentation equipped people with nonreligious arguments they could use to legally define marriage as the union of one man and one woman. I assured him, however, that I did believe in the power of God's word to transform people's lives. After all, God's word is "living and active, sharper than any two-edged sword" (Heb. 4:12), but that does not mean people will always be converted whenever they hear or read it.

The letter to the Hebrews teaches that there were some people in the author's time who heard the preaching of God's promises, but it "did not benefit them, because it did not meet with faith in the hearers" (Heb. 4:2). The book of Acts describes how a servant of the queen of Ethiopia was puzzled when he read the prophecies of the Old Testament. Fortunately, the evangelist Philip came along and asked the servant, "Do you understand what you are reading?" The servant replied, "How can I, unless someone guides me?" (cf. Acts 8:30-31). Philip then showed the servant how the Old Testament's promised Messiah was Jesus Christ.

The biblical authors never claim that their words would always be understood or that they needed no defense. St. Peter even warned his readers that there are confusing passages in Scripture, whose meaning some people twist to their own destruction (2 Peter 3:16). If that's true, then wouldn't Jesus make sure someone like Philip was still around today to help people understand what they're reading in God's word? The fact is, he did do this, through the Church he founded on the apostles. This Church, the Catholic Church, continues to not just preach the Gospel, but also explain and defend it. In that way the Church exists, as St. Paul says, to be "the pillar and bulwark of the truth" (1 Tim. 3:15).

A Better Quote

> ### "No one believes anything unless he is first convinced that it ought to be believed."
> —ST. AUGUSTINE

St. Augustine did not believe that all truths were self-evident, or that people know they are true simply by thinking about them. Some truths are like this (e.g. "I think, therefore I am") but most truths require explanation and even a defense against objections. While Augustine believed that many doctrines could not be known apart from the gift of faith, he also said, "*Nullus quipped credit aliquid nisi prius cogitaverit esse credendum*," or "No one believes anything unless he is first convinced that it ought to be believed."[134]

7. "I believe because it is absurd."

—TERTULLIAN?

"SCIENCE FLIES PEOPLE to the moon, religion flies people into buildings." When I came across this meme on an atheist website I took a breath before trying to charitably explain why this rhetoric doesn't make sense. I pointed out to the other commenters that one could unfairly dismiss science in the same way by saying, "Religion builds hospitals, science builds nerve gas." But trying to refute error on the Internet is like trying to soak up an active oil spill with a Kleenex. The discussion never went anywhere productive. The only redeeming part was that several of the atheists demonstrated exactly how nonbelievers often misunderstand the concept of faith.

Some atheists thought faith and reason mix as well as oil and water because they've heard believers say, "You just have to have faith," or "I believe because I believe." They concluded that faith is belief in the absence of evidence, or even belief *in spite* of evidence. But "faith" just refers to trusting in someone or something (e.g., "I have faith our plane will land safely"); religious faith refers to trusting in God. Some people claim this is a modern view of faith, and that some early Christians had faith in Christianity not just in spite of its absurdities, but *because* of them.

Embracing Absurdity?
Tertullian lived in North Africa in the third century and is often considered the father of Latin or Western Christianity. Even though he became a heretic at the end of his life (which is why he is called an "ecclesial writer" and not a "saint"), his earlier,

orthodox writings are an important witness to the antiquity of the Catholic Faith. But some critics say Tertullian is also an ancient witness to the unreasonableness of the Christian Faith.

In his book *A Devil's Chaplain*, atheist Richard Dawkins likens faith to a malevolent virus that is difficult to cure because its victims ignore its absurdities. When a victim is confronted with parts of their faith that are difficult to understand, they simply call them "mysteries" and ignore them. Dawkins writes, "An extreme symptom of 'mystery is a virtue' infection is Tertullian's '*Certum est quia impossibile est*' (It is certain because it is impossible) [and], "it is by all means to be believed because it is absurd."[135]

The quotes Dawkins refers to come from Tertullian's *De Carne Christi* (*On the Flesh of Christ*), which was a response to the heresy of Docetism. Docetists believed that the incarnate Son, or Jesus Christ, did not possess a real, human body. Instead, he only possessed what *appeared* to be a human body but was actually an illusory or angelic form. Tertullian criticized the Docetists, because if Christ did not have a truly physical, human body, then he could not have died on the cross and atoned for humanity's sins. According to the *Cambridge History of Literary Criticism*:

> Tertullian's writings do not include the words "I believe because it is absurd," and the origin is unknown. The closest to the sentiment in his works is the statement: "The Son of God was crucified: there is no shame, because it is shameful. And the Son of God died: it is believable because it is foolish. And buried, he rose again; it is certain because it is impossible" (*De carne Christi* 5.4).[136]

Tertullian never says, "I believe because it is absurd" (Latin: *Credo quia absurdum*). This appears to be a paraphrase of a line many translators render "It is by all means to be believed, because it is absurd" (Latin: *Prorsus credibile est, quia ineptum est*). The Latin word *absurdum* is not in this passage, so a better translation of the second line would be, "It is credible, because it is foolish." But Tertullian is not arguing that foolish things, on their own, are credible or believable. Tertullian is instead arguing that the first Christians would not have believed God died on a cross and then rose from the dead unless it really happened.

If Jesus was not who he claimed to be, then after the Crucifixion those first potential believers would have thought he was just another failed messiah. They would never have believed Jesus rose from the dead unless they actually saw the risen Jesus. St. Luke even tells us that Jesus "presented himself alive after his passion by many proofs, appearing to [the apostles] during forty days, and speaking of the kingdom of God" (Acts 1:3).

Tertullian's statement, "It is by all means to be believed, because it is absurd," should therefore be understood to mean, "Christianity is true because it's too ridiculous for someone to have simply made up." He did not think God becoming man and dying for our sins was impossible, because in this same work Tertullian wrote, "With God, however, nothing is impossible but what he does not will. Let us consider, then, whether he willed to be born (for if he had the will, he also had the power, and was born)."[137]

The other Tertullian quote critics like to bring up is: "What hath Athens to do with Jerusalem?" This is supposed to prove Tertullian thought that faith (or "Jerusalem") and reason (or "Athens") don't mix, but Tertullian was commenting on St. Paul's warning to not be captivated by "philosophy and empty deceit" (Col. 2:8). Tertullian asks, "What concord is there between the Academy and the Church? What between heretics and Christians?"[138]

Tertullian was not rejecting *all* philosophy. Rather, he rejected particular Greek philosophies that denied the possibility of Christian doctrines like the resurrection of the dead. According to the *Cambridge History of Literary Criticism*, "The older view, that Tertullian was a spokesman for complete separation of Christianity and Classical culture, has in recent years given way to increased recognition in his writings of a synthesis of Christian doctrine with philosophical traditions."[139]

> FAKE
>
> ***"Women should not be enlightened or educated in any way. They should, in fact, be segregated as they are the cause of hideous and involuntary erections in holy men."***
> —ST. AUGUSTINE*?*

Far from being a misogynist, in *City of God* Augustine defended the equal dignity of women with men by refuting the idea that in heaven we would all have male bodies. He writes, "The sex of woman is not a vice, but nature. It shall then indeed be superior to carnal intercourse and child-bearing; nevertheless the female members shall remain adapted not to the old uses, but to a new beauty."[140] He also told a widow he instructed, "What more can I teach you?"[141] which contradicts the idea that women should not be "enlightened or educated in any way."

Augustine did express concern that women's bodies could become objects of lust for men, but a concern about "hideous and involuntary erections" seems to be absent from his writings. It is only mentioned by twenty-first-century authors, none of whom provide a source for the quote, and a search of Augustine's complete works in Latin only yields three uses of the word "erectio," in unrelated contexts.

Flat-Earth Fantasies

Some people attribute the following quote to the sixteenth-century explorer Ferdinand Magellan: "The Church says that the Earth is flat, but I know that it is round. For I have seen the shadow of the earth on the moon and I have more faith in the Shadow than in the Church." But Magellan could not have said this because everyone at that time, including Catholics, knew the earth was round. In fact, most people in the West had known this for thousands of years.

In the second century, Eratosthenes of Cyrene calculated the Earth's circumference at about 85 percent of its actual distance. The ancient Roman historian and scientist Pliny the Elder wrote in A.D. 79, "Everyone agrees that it has the most perfect figure. We always speak of the ball of the Earth, and we admit it to be a globe bounded by the poles."[142] Ancient people knew the earth was round because it explained the earth's curved shadow on the moon and why a ship descends below the horizon as it goes out to sea.

Some Church Fathers, like Lactantius, believed that the Earth was flat, but this was not the majority view and it was never a required view for orthodoxy. According to science historians David Lindberg and Ronald Numbers, "There was scarcely a Christian scholar of the Middle Ages who did not acknowledge [the Earth's] sphericity and even know its approximate circumference."[143]

So what is the source of the flat-Earth myth?

The idea that explorers like Columbus and Magellan faced opposition from the clergy against their plans to circumnavigate the Earth comes from a fictional scene in Washington Irving's *A History of the Life and Voyages of Christopher Columbus* (1828). In reality, those who criticized Columbus's plan to sail to the New World were concerned about the length of the trip, not the shape of the Earth. Columbus grossly underestimated the circumference of the Earth, but was fortunate to find North America where he thought he would find Eastern Asia.

Irving's romanticized portrait of Columbus, with all its historical inaccuracies, found its way into the hands of nineteenth-century secular opponents of the Church. They used the story to liken Christian opponents of Darwinian evolution to ignorant clerics who allegedly denied the Earth was round. One of those critics was Robert Ingersoll, who claimed that Columbus's contemporary Magellan had more faith in a shadow than in the Church, even though there is no record of Magellan ever saying such a thing.[144]

"And yet it moves."
—GALILEO *?*

A popular legend says that after being found guilty of teaching the heresy that the Earth orbited the sun, Galileo muttered under his breath, "*Eppur si muove*"—"And yet it moves." But historian Maurice Finocchiaro calls this account a legend and says it was first told over a century after Galileo's death.[145]

The tale may have its origins in a seventeenth-century Spanish painting depicting Galileo chained up in a dungeon gesturing to a sign that said, "*Eppur si muove*." But after his trial Galileo was not imprisoned in a dungeon—he was placed under house arrest—and there is no record of him ever being tortured.[146] Moreover, Galileo's trial was more focused on his claims that Scripture would have to be reinterpreted. He was not tried for merely holding a heliocentric view of the universe; Copernicus held that view without reprisal decades earlier.

In the twentieth century, Pope St. John Paul II apologized for the Church's treatment of Galileo and said, "The error of the theologians of the time, when they maintained the centrality of the Earth, was to think that our understanding of the physical world's structure was, in some way, imposed by the literal sense of Sacred Scripture."[147]

The Harmony Between Faith and Reason

According to science historian James Hannam, "Atheists and agnostics championed the conflict thesis for their own purposes, but historical research gradually demonstrated that [their sources] had propagated more fantasy than fact in their efforts to prove that science and religion are locked in eternal conflict."[148]

Catholic scientists have contributed to some of the Western world's most important scientific advancements, and the Church made this possible when it created the first universities in the thirteenth century. Notable examples include the seventeenth-century bishop Nicolas Steno who pioneered the study of geology; nineteenth-century Augustinian friar Gregor Mendel, whose experiments with pea plants resulted in what are now known as the Mendelian laws of inheritance; and the Belgian monsignor Georges Lemaître, whose discoveries about the origins of the universe earned him the nickname "Father of the Big Bang theory."

The harmony that exists between faith and reason is beautifully expressed in the opening lines of Pope St. John Paul II's encyclical *Fides et ratio* (*On Faith and Reason*). He writes, "Faith and reason are like two wings on which the human spirit rises to the contemplation of truth." The *Catechism* also explains why faith and reason can never contradict one another:

> Though faith is above reason, there can never be any real discrepancy between faith and reason. Since the same God who reveals mysteries and infuses faith has bestowed the light of reason on the human mind, God cannot deny himself, nor can truth ever contradict truth. Consequently, methodical research in all branches of knowledge, provided it is carried out in a truly scientific manner and does not override moral laws, can never conflict with the faith, because

the things of the world and the things of faith derive from the same God (283).

The Catholic teaching on faith and reason avoids the heresy of rationalism, which says that we should only believe what can be proved from reason, and the heresy of fideism, which claims that what we believe need not be proved by reason or cannot be proved by reason. Regarding fideism, the First Vatican Council condemned the idea that "the one, true God, our creator and lord, cannot be known with certainty from the things that have been made, by the natural light of human reason."[149]

Even if someone doesn't have faith, or a trust in God, he can still know God exists by using reason to conclude that there must be an ultimate and infinite explanation of the world. The *Catechism* tells us that while the gift of faith is necessary to have an intimate relationship with God, "The proofs of God's existence, however, can predispose one to faith and help one to see that faith is not opposed to reason" (35).

Misunderstanding Mysteries

Even though God's existence can be known by reason alone, this does not mean that every truth about God can be known by reason alone. Man could never know, for example, that God is a Trinity of Father, Son, and Holy Spirit if God had not revealed this truth in Sacred Scripture and Sacred Tradition. Since this truth of the Faith cannot be known by reason alone, it is one of several doctrines that are called mysteries.[150] But for an atheist like Richard Dawkins, calling something a theological "mystery" is just an excuse to avoid explaining what seems to be unexplainable:

> Calling it a Mystery makes everything OK, you see. At least, it works for a mind well prepared by background infection.

Exactly the same trick is performed in the "Mystery" of the Trinity. Mysteries are not meant to be solved, they are meant to strike awe. The "mystery is a virtue" idea comes to the aid of the Catholic who would otherwise find intolerable the obligation to believe the obvious nonsense of the transubstantiation [sic] and the "three-in-one."[151]

Contrary to Dawkins's assertions, the Catholic Church does not describe something as a mystery in order to stifle reasoned discussion about it. Theologians have been discussing mysteries like the Trinity for centuries and continue to do so in theology journals and classrooms today. Rather, calling some article of faith a mystery shows it is a part of divine revelation. Since these doctrines relate to the infinite majesty of God, they cannot be fully contained in our finite intellects. They can be understood at a basic level, but we can never exhaust depths of these parts of the Faith through our finite explorations of them.

The term "mystery" can even be applied to scientific descriptions of things like the inside of a black hole or the condition of the universe right after the Big Bang. Scientists have a general idea of what black holes and the big bang are like, but since we've never seen either of them we must admit that a complete understanding of these realities lie beyond our grasp. Supernatural realities, like the Trinity, are even more elusive because they do not lie within the physical universe and so they can't be explored with things like microscopes and telescopes. Instead, they must be explored with conceptual models, just like other unobservable philosophical and scientific concepts like infinity or higher physical dimensions.

St. Augustine, St. Thomas Aquinas, and Pope Benedict XVI have each proposed models or descriptions of the Trinity that help us better understand this doctrine.[152] These models do not fully reveal what the Trinity is like any more than a map of the Grand Canyon fully reveals what the Grand Canyon is like to someone who has never been there. But, like a map of the wilderness, theological explanations are a useful guide that helps us understand the boundary and nature of God's majesty. They help us better perceive God when we contemplate the mysteries of our Faith.

Reason is capable of shining a light on the mysteries of the faith, but our comprehension of these truths will be limited until we experience God in heavenly glory in the next life. St. Paul put it this way: "For now we see in a mirror dimly, but then face to face. Now I know in part; then I shall understand fully, even as I have been fully understood" (1 Cor. 13:12).

A Better Quote

> **"The difficulty of explaining, 'why I am a Catholic' is that there are ten thousand reasons all amounting to one reason: that Catholicism is true."**
> —G.K. CHESTERTON[153]

G.K. Chesterton has been called "the apostle of common sense" because of his insightful, witty defenses of the Catholic faith. For Chesterton, faith was not something you merely chose on a whim or believed because of an emotional feeling. Instead, it was something your mind could firmly grasp as a foundation for living.

The Catholic faith doesn't just make sense—the world becomes senseless without it. Chesterton also praised the humility of those who see the limits of their own reasoning abilities and are willing to learn from the Church Christ gave us. He put it this way, "A Catholic is a person who has plucked up courage to face the incredible and inconceivable idea that something else may be wiser than he is."[154]

8. "Rome has spoken, the case is closed."

—ST. AUGUSTINE?

ONCE, DURING A formal debate between a Protestant apologist and a Catholic priest, the priest reminded the audience that the early Church did not believe in the Protestant doctrine of sola scriptura. Rather, the early Christians believed in the authority of the Church to be the custodian of God's Word in Sacred Scripture and Sacred Tradition. He cited St. Augustine as believing this, because St. Augustine allegedly said, "*Roma locuta est, causa finita est*," or "Rome has spoken, the case is closed."

The Protestant apologist immediately interrupted the priest and asked, "Sir, can you tell me where that's found?" The priest started to stammer and the Protestant apologist continued, "You just made a quotation from Augustine and I'm challenging you. That is said to appear in Sermon 131, but that is one of the most common errors among Roman Catholic apologists."[155]

It's true that Augustine did not say the exact words, "Rome has spoken, the case is closed." But, he did say something similar that serves as evidence for the authority of the Catholic Church. In order to understand what Augustine said, we have to return to the Pelagian controversy we discussed a few chapters ago.

"Here I stand; I can do no other."
—MARTIN LUTHER*?*

This could be considered the Protestant retort to the idea that once "Rome has spoken" a cause or belief is finished. Most histories of the Reformation claim that at the Diet of Worms Catholic officials gave Luther a chance to renounce his heretical views. Luther instead chose to double down on them and defiantly proclaimed at the end of a passionate speech, "Here I stand; I can do no other."

Diarmaid MacCulloch says, in his classic study of the Reformation, that these words "have become the most memorable thing Luther never said."[156] Luther's speech at Worms did happen, but this particular line probably comes from Georg Rorer, the first editor of Luther's collected works, and not from Luther himself.

The Case Is Closed?

In 415, a regional synod of bishops in Africa condemned the teachings of Pelagius's disciple Caelestius. The regional Council of Carthage also condemned Caelestius, and Pope Innocent III confirmed this decision. Pelagius and Caelestius, however, refused to accept the councils' condemnations and made a direct appeal to the pope. But Pope Innocent I died in 417, before he received their appeal, so the matter fell into the hands of his successor, Pope Zosimus.

Zosimus personally met with Caelestius, and after receiving letters from both men that claimed they still accepted the teachings of the Catholic Church, Zosimus reversed their excommunications. However, both letters were dishonest and hid the men's true heretical theologies. Pelagius and Caelestius simply wanted their excommunications lifted so they could spread their heresies throughout the Church. Caelestius in particular, wanted the pope to overrule letters the bishop of Constantinople sent warning churches in Greece and western Asia about his teachings. Philip Schaff, a Protestant writer who is very critical of the Catholic Church, admits an act of deception occurred: "[Augustine] opposed Pope Zosimus, when, deceived by Pelagius, he declared him sound in the faith."[157]

Augustine, along with the other African bishops who were more familiar with these heretics, realized that the pope had been duped. They urged Zosimus to reconsider his ruling, and Augustine commented on the matter in his 131st sermon: "Already on this matter two councils have sent to the Apostolic See, whence also rescripts [reports] have come. The cause is finished [Latin: *causa finita est*]; would that the error also be finished!"

What he meant was that two African councils, one in Carthage and another in Mileve, sent decisions on the Pelagian heresy to Pope Innocent. Rescripts (or reports) from the pope came back that unequivocally condemned Pelagianism and confirmed the excommunications of Pelagius and Caelestius. However, the pope did leave room for the men to return to the Faith if they were to "recover from the snares of the devil." This corresponds to other times in Church history when heretics and notorious sinners repented and were restored to communion with the Church before their deaths.

Pope Zosimus did not contradict Church teaching because he did not define Pelagianism to be orthodox. Instead, he chose to lift an ecclesial punishment that seemed to have been meted out unfairly. But once Pope Zosimus was made aware of Pelagius's and Caelestius's deceptions, he reversed his decision and reinstated the men's justly deserved punishments.

It's true Augustine did not say "Rome has spoken," but he did say the Apostolic See, or the bishop of Rome, had given reports on the Pelagian matter. "Rome has spoken, the case is closed" became a paraphrase for "The Apostolic See has issued reports, the case is closed." Augustine did say *"Causa finita est"* because the cause of Pelagianism was finished when the bishop of Rome confirmed the decisions of the African councils that had condemned it. The matter only continued because, unlike heresies, people can repent, and so the issue of receiving Pelagius and Caelestius back into the Church still had to be resolved.

While this episode demonstrates the unique authority of the Church and the bishop of Rome, I don't recommend citing it as evidence of Augustine's belief in the Church's authority. In doing so, one runs the risk of turning the discussion into a debate about what Augustine "actually said" and getting bogged down in historical minutiae. Instead, I recommend sharing Augustine's reply to the heretic Manichaeus, when he said, "I should not believe the gospel except as moved by the authority of the Catholic Church."

Manichaeus rejected the authority of Catholic bishops like Augustine, but the bishop of Hippo showed Manichaeus that such a rejection undermined his own beliefs. The Manicheans were fond of trying to prove their heretical doctrines from Scripture alone, but this led to the question of why anyone, be they orthodox or heretical, should trust the Bible in the first place. Augustine posed this challenge:

> Perhaps you will read the gospel to me, and will attempt to find there a testimony to Manichaeus. But should you meet with a person not yet believing the gospel, how would you reply to him were he to say, "I do not believe?" For my part, I should not believe the gospel except as moved by the authority of the Catholic Church.[158]

Augustine then said Manichaeus was trapped between the horns of a dilemma. If Manichaeus said, "Believe the Catholics," or in other words, "Trust the Catholic Church against those who deny the authority of the Gospels," then part of that trust includes accepting the Church's rejection of heretics like Manichaeus. On the other hand, if Manicheaus said, "Do not believe the Catholics" then Manichaeus couldn't use the gospels to prove his heresy was true because, according to Augustine, "it was at the command of the Catholics that I believed the gospel."[159]

This undermines the Protestant claim that God's revelation is found in Scripture alone (sola scriptura) and that Scripture authenticates its own authority.[160] The early Church did not believe in sola scriptura, as evidenced in the second-century writings of St. Irenaeus, who wonders what would have happened if the apostles had not left behind any sacred writings. He says, "Would it not be necessary, [in that case], to follow the course of the tradition which they handed down to those to whom they did commit the Churches?"[161]

"In necessary things, unity; in doubtful things, liberty; in all things, charity."
—ST. AUGUSTINE?

The sentiment behind this quote is commendable, but the earliest citation of it comes from the seventeenth century, and it is not attributed to Augustine.[162] Pope John XXIII said, "The common saying, expressed in various ways *and attributed to various authors* [emphasis added], must be recalled with approval: in essentials, unity; in doubtful matters, liberty; in all things, charity."[163]

Infallible Dogmas

When it comes to obeying the teachings of the Church there are two extremes. On the one hand are the so-called "cafeteria Catholics" who pick and choose which doctrines they will or won't accept. Their motto is, "Rome has spoken, but the case is always open." On the other hand, some Catholics believe that everything the Church teaches or everything the pope says is an infallible, unchangeable teaching and it can never be questioned. Some skeptics say this means Catholics must even believe unreasonable things since St. Ignatius of Loyola said, "To find the right way in everything, we must always hold the following: the white I see I shall believe to be black, if the Hierarchical Church so decides the matter."[164]

But the reality lies between these views and is best understood when we examine the difference between dogma, doctrine, and discipline.

The central teachings of our faith are called dogmas and they demand our most committed level of belief, or what is called the assent of faith (CCC 891). The Vatican's Congregation for the Doctrine of the Faith says of dogmas: "Whoever obstinately places them in doubt or denies them falls under the censure of heresy, as indicated by the respective canons of the Codes of Canon Law." According to the *Catechism*:

> The Church's Magisterium exercises the authority it holds from Christ to the fullest extent when it defines dogmas, that is, when it proposes, in a form obliging the Christian people to an irrevocable adherence of faith, truths contained in divine revelation or also when it proposes, in a definitive way, truths having a necessary connection with these. (88)

The Church's infallible teachings only extend to matters of faith and morals. So those who cite St. Ignatius' discussion of colors don't realize that he was using hyperbole to make a point: because Christ founded the Church what it definitively teaches about divine revelation should be trusted over our own opinions—no matter how strong they may be on a certain matter.[165]

This assent of faith also includes assent to truths that are not a part of divine revelation but have a necessary connection to it. For example, there is nothing in divine revelation that speaks about popes or general councils from after the apostolic age, but truths about papal elections or the validity of general councils have a necessary connection to the dogma of the Church's general infallibility that is found in divine revelation.

According to the Church's canon law, a teaching is not infallible unless the Church explicitly says it is infallible (*Codex Iuris Canonici*, 749.3). That happens when the pope speaks in his capacity as the successor of St. Peter and defines a dogma, such as when Pope Pius XII defined the dogma of Mary's Assumption in 1950. Dogmas can also be defined by the canons of an ecumenical council or by the ordinary and universal teaching authority of the Church, such as through the universal witness in ecclesial documents that killing innocent human beings is wrong.

Because the pope is capable of defining a dogma, some people think he cannot make any mistakes or can never be corrected, but that isn't true. The dogma of papal infallibility only applies when, "as supreme pastor and teacher of all the faithful—who confirms his brethren in the faith [the pope] proclaims by a definitive act a doctrine pertaining to faith or morals" (CCC 891). This means the pope is protected from error when he formally defines a dogma that is related to faith or morals. The pope can err when he speaks as a private theologian or even when he is teaching but not making a dogmatic definition.

"We have made a goddess of the blessed Virgin . . . Save the church from the shipwreck which threatens her, asking from the holy Scriptures alone for the rule of faith."
—BISHOP JOSIP STROSSMAYER**?**

Some people claim that at the First Vatican Council bishop Josip Strossmayer criticized the decision to formally define the dogma of papal infallibility. Bishop Strossmayer did oppose defining the dogma in a formal speech, but he later supported the council's vote on the matter. After the council, a former priest named José Agustín de Escudero created a forged version of Bishop Strossmayer's speech that was an anti-Catholic tract in disguise.[166]

In the fourteenth century, Pope John XXII erroneously taught in some of his sermons that the saints in heaven do not see the beatific vision of God until the final judgment. This did not detract from his exercise of papal infallibility, because the pope did not require the faithful to accept this belief and it was not formally defined as an error until after his death. Pope John XXII was willing to be corrected by other theologians, and he abandoned this belief before his death in 1334.[167]

Another example of papal correction occurred in the same century, when Catherine of Siena pleaded with Pope Gregory XI to return the papacy to Rome after it had been in exile in Avignon, France, for almost seventy years. She said to him, "I beg of you, on behalf of Christ crucified, that you be not a timorous child but manly. Open your mouth and swallow down the bitter for the sweet."[168] St. Paul even had to correct St. Peter when the latter chose not to dine with Gentiles out of fear of offending fellow Jewish Christians (Gal. 2:14-2:16).

The pope is protected from formally binding the Church to error, but he can still personally err. If this happens, he may require moral or theological correction, but this does not refute the dogma of papal infallibility. In fact, nothing can nullify Christ's promise that "the gates of Hades" shall not prevail against the Church and cause her as a whole to fall into moral or theological error.

Proposed Doctrines

Doctrine is teaching that the Church proposes for the faithful to believe. It can refer to an individual teaching (a doctrine) or to the totality of all the Church's teachings (Catholic doctrine). Even though every dogma of the Faith is a doctrine, most doctrines are not dogmas, nor are they infallibly defined. They can be changed or clarified, and so they require "religious submission of mind and will" rather than the assent of faith.

Consider this teaching from the *Catechism*: "The Church teaches that every spiritual soul is created immediately by God—it is not 'produced' by the parents—and also that it is immortal: it does not perish when it separates from the body at death, and it will be reunited with the body at the final resurrection" (366).

That human beings have immortal souls is a dogma of the Church that was infallibly defined at the Fifth Lateran Council in 1513 (it has also been part of the continual, universal teaching of the Church, or the "ordinary Magisterium"). That God creates those souls directly, however, is a doctrine rather than a dogma. The Church could declare this to be a dogma in the future, but for now it is a doctrine because it has not been infallibly defined as being divinely revealed. Helpful guides to which Catholic doctrines are dogmas can be found in Ludwig Ott's *Fundamentals of Catholic Dogma* and Henry Denzinger's *The Sources of Catholic Dogma*.

The faithful cannot openly dissent against any doctrine, but unlike dogma, it is not a grave sin to personally fail to accept a doctrine that has not been infallibly defined. Still, it is a serious matter to withhold the submission of the mind and will, and the Church usually speaks of this happening among theologians who, after careful study, cautiously help the Magisterium better understand a disputed issue. St. Teresa of Avila, who is one of only thirty-five people who hold the title Doctor of the Church, expressed her loyalty to the Church this way: "It will be the fault of ignorance, not malice, if I say anything contrary to the doctrine of the Holy Roman Catholic Church."[169]

CLOSE, BUT NOT QUITE

"I don't need a church to tell me I'm wrong where I already know I'm wrong; I need a church to tell me I'm wrong where I think I'm right."
—G.K. CHESTERTON**?**

In his essay "The Catholic Church and Conversion," Chesterton wrote about contemporary religions and philosophies that touted their newness and popular support as virtues. He argued in response that novelty and popular support are not the hallmarks of the one, true faith, saying, "We do not really want a religion that is right where we are right. What we want is a religion that is right where we are wrong."[170]

The difference between the assent of faith and the religious submission of mind and will is not a license for Catholics to reject any noninfallible teachings they simply do not like. It is instead a recognition that the Church does not always make its teaching definitive, but the faithful should still trust in the shepherds Christ has left us. This should be done even as they, under the guidance of the Holy Spirit, further clarify and present the Faith handed on to them that they pass on to us (cf. 2 Tim. 2:2).

There are also theological issues and questions to which

the Church has not proposed a definitive answer or doctrine. Until the Church does, it may permit a variety of theological opinions or speculations on a matter without officially endorsing any of them. For example, while Mary's Assumption has been dogmatically defined, the Church has not settled the question of whether she was assumed into heaven before or after death, and allows Catholics to hold either view (though the latter is the more traditional view).

Authoritative Discipline

Disciplines are the rules and laws the Church proposes by the authority given to it by Christ. Even though disciplines can be changed, the faithful are still obliged to obey them, just as citizens must obey speed limits that a municipal government can change when it deems necessary. Some people think that disciplines are as unchanging as dogmas, and that if they change, it constitutes disobedience to previous Church teaching.

For example, in 1570 Pope Pius V issued the apostolic constitution *Quo Primum*, which promulgated the Tridentine liturgy for the Mass. This liturgy was celebrated in Latin with the priest facing the altar and was the ordinary form of the Mass until Pope Paul VI promulgated the new order of the Mass (the "novus ordo") in 1969.

Some Catholics who are critical of the new form of the Mass say it is invalid because Pope Pius V said of the Tridentine Mass in *Quo Primum*, "We grant and concede in perpetuity that, for the chanting or reading of the Mass in any church whatsoever, this Missal is hereafter to be followed absolutely."[171] However, Pope Pius V's declaration on the liturgy meant the new liturgy had to be followed unless someone with proper authority, including the current or future pope, changed it.

In the Old Covenant, God commanded that worship on Saturday, or the Sabbath, was to be "a perpetual covenant" (Exod. 31:16), but this did not prevent him from commanding worship be offered on the Lord's Day, or Sunday, in the New Covenant (CCC 2175). Likewise, canon law states that the pope, "By virtue of his office . . . possesses supreme, full, immediate, and universal ordinary power in the Church, which he is always able to exercise freely" (CIC 331).

If a previous pope could forever bind the Church to a particular discipline, then the current pope would not possess "supreme, full, immediate, and universal" jurisdiction over Christ's Church. *Quo Primum* itself included exceptions for churches where "there has prevailed a custom of a similar kind," and those churches did not have to adopt the new Tridentine missal. This shows that Catholic disciplines can be modified or even suspended (which is done through a dispensation) for the good of the Church and her members. In fact, in his 2007 apostolic letter *Summorum Pontificum*, Pope Benedict XVI extended the ability of priests to celebrate the older Tridentine form of the Mass.

To summarize, "when Rome speaks," it may propose doctrine, or teachings to which we should submit the mind and will. Some of these doctrines are dogmas that are unchangeable and, because they are part of divine revelation, they require the assent of faith, which it is gravely sinful to withhold. Disciplines, on the other hand, come from the Church's God-given authority and must be obeyed even though the Magisterium can alter or abolish them at any time. Since the Church issues different kinds of teachings, we should not simplistically say, "When Rome speaks, the case is closed," but rather, "When Rome speaks, the faithful should carefully listen and obey."

A Better Quote

> *"He can no longer have God for his Father,
> who has not the Church for his mother."*
> —ST. CYPRIAN OF CARTHAGE[172]

The Church fathers, who are the most influential Christian writers of the first part of the Church's history, agreed that God did not merely give us Scripture as our source of authority. In the third century St. Cyprian of Carthage wrote several treatises on the unity of the Catholic Church, which he found rooted in its particular apostolic connections.

For example, he wrote in the first edition of *On the Unity of the Church*, "A primacy is given to Peter, whereby it is made clear that there is but one Church and one chair. . . . If he desert the chair of Peter upon whom the Church was built, can he still be confident that his is in the Church?"[173]

The ancient witnesses that testify to the Church being an enduring, visible reality with a hierarchy whose supreme pastor is the Bishop of Rome, the successor of St. Peter, brings to mind the words of Cardinal Henry Newman, "To be deep in history is to cease to be Protestant."[174]

9. "The road to hell is paved with the bones of priests."

—ST. JOHN CHRYSOSTOM?

BENEATH THE CHURCH of Santa Maria della Concezione dei Cappuccini in the city of Rome is a gruesome sight: a crypt full of bones from over 3,700 bodies. This isn't the scene of a war crime, but a place where Capuchin friars have laid members of their order to rest since the seventeenth century. When my wife and I saw this crypt on our honeymoon (aren't I romantic?), we marveled at the intricate displays of the bones in each crypt. As we walked through the crypt, I stumbled across a sign posted above a series of skeletons. It read: "What you are now, we once were; what we are now, you shall be."

Sometimes we can be so caught up with the mundane details of this life that we forget to plan where we want to be in the next life. This brings us to our next apocryphal quote, this time from St. John Chrysostom, who describes the absolute last place you'd want to spend eternity: "The road to hell is paved with the bones of priests and monks, and the skulls of bishops are the lampposts that light the path."

An Ecclesial Highway to Hell?

Some sources attribute a variant of this quote to St. Athanasius, who goes further than Chrysostom by saying, "The floor to hell is paved with the skulls of priests." However, these descriptions of hell sound more like the medieval author Dante Alighieri than any of the early Church Fathers. In fact, the earliest connection between this quote and St.

John Chrysostom comes from the Protestant Reformer John Wesley, who said, "A lifeless, unconverting minister is the murder-general of his parish . . . I could not have blamed St. Chrysostom, if he had only said, 'Hell is paved with the skulls of such Christian priests!'"[175] I've seen online commenters share this alleged Chrysostom quote when stories appear about priests who have fallen into temptation, which I find to be very smug and unhelpful. It's kind of a "See, I told you those priests can't be trusted!" But Chrysostom never claimed that all the clergy would end up as fixtures on some metaphorical highway to hell, even though he worried about their souls. In his commentary on Acts of the Apostles he writes, "The soul of a Bishop is for all the world like a vessel in a storm: lashed from every side, by friends, by foes, by one's own people, by strangers . . . I do not think there are many among Bishops that will be saved, but many more that perish."[176]

The authors of the New Testament expressed a similar concern for the clergy. James 3:1 says, "Let not many of you become teachers, my brethren, for you know that we who teach shall be judged with greater strictness." In his letter to Timothy, St. Paul said, "If any one aspires to the office of bishop, he desires a noble task." He then gave Timothy a litany of requirements for anyone who would hold this office and warned against ordaining those who were recent converts or couldn't manage their own households. Paul feared that if one of these men were ordained, "he may be puffed up with conceit and fall into the condemnation of the devil" or "he may fall into reproach and the snare of the devil" (1 Tim. 3:6-7).

I once spoke with a woman who struggled reconciling her Catholic faith with the clergy abuse scandal.[177] She asked, "If they're really men of God in Christ's Church, then how could they do that?"

I responded, "Let me ask you, does the devil hate Christ's Church?"

"Absolutely!"

"Then of all the members of the Church, who is he going to attack the most?"

She thought for a moment and then said, "The priests!" This echoes St. John Vianney, the patron saint of priests, who said, "When people want to destroy religion they begin by attacking the priest; for when there is no priest, there is no sacrifice: and when there is no sacrifice, there is no religion."[178]

When we hear about scandal involving the clergy we shouldn't casually dismiss it, but neither should we feel ashamed of our faith as a whole. Rather, scandal can be an opportunity to reflect on the spiritual attacks every believer faces. St. Peter warned, "Be sober, be watchful. Your adversary the devil prowls around like a roaring lion, seeking someone to devour. Resist him, firm in your faith" (1 Pet. 5:8-9).

It is also a reminder that we should pray for one another and encourage one another in practical ways. In his letter to the Galatians, Paul said, "If a man is overtaken in any trespass, you who are spiritual should restore him in a spirit of gentleness. Look to yourself, lest you too be tempted. Bear one another's burdens, and so fulfill the law of Christ" (Gal. 6:1-2). We should especially offer up prayers for priests so that they can bear the unique burdens they face as the shepherds of Christ's flock. This prayer from Pope Benedict XVI is a great example:

> Lord Jesus Christ . . . Grant that all who are ordained to the ministerial priesthood may be ever more conformed to you, the divine Master. May they preach the Gospel with pure heart and clear conscience . . . Through the prayers of the blessed Virgin Mary, your Mother and ours, draw all priests and the flocks entrusted to their care to the fullness of eternal life, where you live and reign with the Father and the Holy Spirit, one God, for ever and ever. Amen[179]

PROBABLY FAKE

"If in 1,800 years we clergy have failed to destroy the Church, do you really think that you'll be able to do it?"
—CARDINAL ERCOLE CONSALVI?
(said to Napoleon Bonaparte, after the general had threatened to crush the Catholic Church)

Cardinal Ercole Consalvi was involved in the 1801 concordat between Napoleon and the Church, so it is not outside the realm of possibility that such an exchange took place. However, the earliest description of the story I could find was in a 1972 article in the *New York Times*. It said that when Napoleon "warned that he could destroy the church, Consalvi replied that not even the priests had been able to do that."[180] But the anecdote does not appear in the 1908 *Catholic Encyclopedia* entry about Cardinal Consalvi, and Louis Antoine Fauvelet de Bourrienne, who recorded Napoleon's memoirs, does not record the incident either.[181]

The Sinner's Hospital

In my book *Why We're Catholic*, I described the embarrassment I felt after my conversion to the Catholic faith when the clergy abuse scandal began making headlines. I wrote:

> It feels like a punch to the gut when something or someone you care about is caught up in scandal. You may even be tempted to cut off all association with a scandalized group or person and try to make a fresh start. But as St. Augustine is reported to have said, "The Church is not a hotel for saints, it is a hospital for sinners." The issue is not whether the patients are sinners, or even if the staff are sinners. The issue is whether the hospital (or the Church) has the cure for sin that has infected everyone.[182]

You'll notice that I wrote, "St. Augustine is reported to have said, 'The Church is not a hotel for saints, it is a hospital for sinners.'" I agree with the message behind that quote, but even then I was skeptical that it came from Augustine. At that time public hospitals were still in their infancy and primarily located in the Eastern Empire, far away from Augustine. Most people also rarely traveled far enough to justify the common use of inns, let alone "hotels," which did not yet exist.

The earliest source I have found for this quote is a 1931 address from Episcopal bishop George Stewart. In one passage, Stewart addressed people who say "I love Christ, but I hate the Church," and "There are too many hypocrites in the Church." Stewart responded by pointing out that Christ established a Church, and so those who love and follow Christ will love and follow his Church. He notes how Jesus selected twelve apostles to form "the nucleus of an organization which has swept out and down the centuries proclaiming the good news of the Son." Concerning hypocrisy, he said:

> I know it has been full of sinners. What did you think the Church was, a club for shining saints? But if it has been a hospital for sinners, it has also been a training school for saints, who have been disciplined and trained in her fellowship not as men in barracks but as soldiers on the march.[183]

A similar idea can be found in a 1964 "Dear Abby" advice column featuring a couple who had been cohabiting for decades and wanted to regularize their relationship. The couple's friends and neighbors think they are legally married, so they ask Abby (Abigail Van Buren) for advice on how to locate a church far away that does not have a waiting period for issuing marriage licenses. They also say, "We do not belong to a church because we do not feel we are worthy of going to church," to which Van Buren responds:

The very fact that you are troubled by the way you have been living proves that you are worthy of going to church. A church is not a museum for saints—it's a hospital for sinners. Go to a clergyman whether you belong to a church now or not, and let him chart your course. You will be amazed at how easily you can legalize your union quietly, without publicity. Good luck.[184]

While the quote may come from the twentieth century, its message can be traced back to Jesus' ministry. For example, when the Pharisees and scribes criticized Jesus for dining with sinners, he said to them, "Those who are well have no need of a physician, but those who are sick; I came not to call the righteous, but sinners" (Mark 2:17).

MISATTRIBUTED

"Those who love the barque of Peter ought to stay out of the engine room."
—JOHN CARDINAL HENRY NEWMAN?

The quote actually comes from the British Catholic apologist Msgr. Ronald Knox. Although it is not found in his extant writings, in her biography of the Knox brothers, Knox's niece Penelope Fitzgerald recalls him saying it. She writes, "'He who travels in the barque of St. Peter,' Ronnie once said, 'had better not look too closely into the engine-room.'"[185] The quotation appears in a description of the English bishops' hesitation in approving Knox's new translation of the Bible.

Hypocrisy and Cheap Grace

Some people do give Christians the reputation for being hypocrites, but only those people who don't understand the gospel. For example, Christians who believe in "once saved, always saved" think that nothing can cost them their salvation; they believe that even if a Christian became an atheistic serial killer he would still be saved. Charles Stanley, a defender of this view, claims that a Christian will usually ask God to forgive him of serious sins, but "even if he does not, the fact remains that he is forgiven!"[186]

Research from Georgia State University shows that some prisoners think God has to forgive them even if they aren't sorry for their wrongdoing. One of the study's subjects, a twenty-five-year-old criminal nicknamed "Cool," always says a "quick little prayer" before committing a crime in order to "stay cool with Jesus."[187] This may seem like an extreme case, but I've heard people justify serious sins like abortion and adultery by saying prior to the act, "It's between me and God and he understands what I'm going through so he'll forgive me."

This is what the Protestant pastor and Holocaust victim Dietrich Bonhoeffer called "cheap grace," or "grace without discipleship." It is a feel-good message that divorces God's forgiveness from the necessity of man's repentance. According to Bonhoeffer, when this "gospel" is preached it basically says, "Of course you have sinned, but now everything is forgiven, so you can stay as you are and enjoy the consolations of forgiveness."[188]

Bonhoeffer contrasts this with "costly grace," or the gift of salvation that demands submission to God as the ultimate authority in our lives. He writes of this grace: "It is costly because it compels a man to submit to the yoke of Christ and follow him; it is grace because Jesus says: 'My yoke is easy and my burden is light.'"[189] The cost of this grace is high not because we must do anything to earn it, but because we are often tempted to reject it.

"What's Wrong with the world? Dear sirs, I am."
—G.K. CHESTERTON?

According to a popular story about G.K. Chesterton, the *Times* of London sent out a request for writers to answer the question, "What's wrong with the world?" The shortest reply came from Chesterton, who simply wrote, "I am." The story is one of the best-known anecdotes about Chesterton, but there is little or no evidence that he actually wrote a letter like that or that the *Times* ever asked writers to answer that question.

The American Chesterton Society "suspects it is true" because it is retold so much, but they also admit, "What we have not found, however, is any documentary evidence for it."[190] Chesterton did compose an anthology called *What's Wrong with the World?* but it makes no mention of answering a newspaper query (which would be odd if that was the source of the anthology's title). What's more likely is the title of Chesterton's anthology served as the inspiration for the apocryphal "Dear sirs, I am" story.

However, if a Christian does reject it and fall into sin, that does not prove he is a hypocrite. That's because hypocrisy is not the same thing as failure, and a hypocrite is not a person who says one thing but does another. Are people whose New Year's resolutions include daily exercise hypocrites when they stop going to the gym in March? When a mother tells her child to say "please" and "thank you," but fails to do the same on a busy Monday morning, is she a hypocrite? Usually not, because hypocrisy is not just the failure to live up to one's own standards; it is also the active effort to hide one's true self from other people.

The English word "hypocrite" comes from the Greek word *hypokrites*, which originally referred to stage actors.[191] In ancient Greece actors wore masks to signify which character they were playing, and as time went on, a hypocrite represented someone who wore a figurative mask. They didn't merely say one thing and do another; they said one thing and *believed* another. The politician who extols family values but gets caught having an affair may be a hypocrite if he doesn't really believe in those values and just espouses them to get votes. But if he does believe in them and still has an affair, then he's an example of a human vulnerable to temptation that believers must shield themselves against.

In his first letter to the Corinthians, St. Paul compared Christians to athletes and noted that while the latter compete for a crown made of olive wreaths, the former strive for an imperishable crown of salvation. Paul says our spiritual lives require just as much self-control as an athlete's training regiment, and he says of himself, "I pommel my body and subdue it, lest after preaching to others I myself should be disqualified" (1 Cor. 9:27). In a similar vein, St. Josemaría Escrivá, the founder of Opus Dei, compared the life of a saint to an athlete who never lets defeat keep him from the prize he seeks:

> The ascetical struggle is not something negative and therefore hateful, but rather a joyful affirmation. It is a sport. A good sportsman doesn't fight to gain just one victory, and that at the first attempt. He has to build himself up for it, training over a long period of time, calmly and confidently. He keeps trying again and again, and if he doesn't succeed at the first attempt, he keeps on trying with determination until the obstacle is overcome. [192]

In the unpublished sequel to his autobiography, Nelson Mandela said he did not like being considered a saint. He writes, "I never was one, even on the basis of an earthly definition of a saint as a sinner who keeps on trying."[193] Escrivá is often credited with saying "a saint is a sinner who keeps on trying," and though he did not write those specific words, he did offer this similar encouragement: "Don't forget that the saint is not the person who never falls, but rather the one who never fails to get up again, humbly and with a holy stubbornness."[194]

Canonized saints are those people the Church recognizes to be in heaven, but the Bible says all members of the body of Christ are saints (Col. 1:1-2), or "holy ones" (Greek, *hagioi*). A "holy one" or "saint" is a person who is set apart and called by Christ to be in communion with him and his Church. What makes a person a saint in this life is not an absence of sin, but a response to sin that always turns back to God in humble surrender. This response trusts in God's mercy and forgiveness, because a saint believes God's grace is sufficient to overcome any obstacle to holiness. What the Lord told Paul is true for all of us: "My grace is sufficient for you, for my power is made perfect in weakness" (2 Cor. 12:9).

A Better Quote

"You cannot be half a saint. You must be a whole saint or no saint at all."
—ST. THÉRÈSE OF LISIEUX

In 1897, St. Thérèse composed a reply to a young priest named Maurice Bellière while she was dying of tuberculosis. Bellière often dwelt on his past sins and worried that he was not capable of serving God in his foreign missions. St. Thérèse reassured him that God is a father who loves his children and prepares them for anything he asks of them. We should not let a fear of looking like a hypocrite or failure hold us back from our vocation to sanctity. In one of her letters she writes:

"Sometimes Jesus delights 'to reveal his secrets to the little ones': as an example, when I had read your first letter of 15 October 1895, I thought the same thing as your director. You cannot be half a saint, you must be a whole saint or no saint at all . . . The remembrance of my faults humiliates me, leads me never to rely at all on my strength, which is only weakness; but the remembrance speaks to me still more of mercy and love. When one casts one's faults into the consuming flame of Love, how could they fail to be consumed past return?"[195]

10. "God is always trying to give good things to us, but our hands are too full to receive them."

—ST. AUGUSTINE?

As I STARED at the clock above the door of the ballroom, I knew I was going to waste most of my Saturday. A week earlier I approached a couple at my office to ask them if they would like to donate to a mission trip I was leading. They said they would consider giving to me if I accompanied them to a motivational seminar at which I could learn to "achieve my dreams."

I figured if this is what it would take to get their support, then why not? Two hours into the seminar the leader asked each of us to come up with different ways to cross the room in order to show we have "the power inside" to solve any problem. I didn't want to disappoint the couple who invited me, or lie about a family emergency, so I stayed until the bitter end.

The remaining five hours were just platitudes and endless appeals to spend three thousand dollars to go to a weekend-long "super seminar" in another state. One of those "feel-good" slogans that stayed with me was attributed to St. Augustine: "God is always trying to give good things to us, but our hands are too full to receive them."

In other words, until you unleash "the power inside," God won't give you the success your heart desires. I've seen this quote justify New-Age concepts like centering prayer and the enneagram, but it's especially popular with a theology I loathe: the "prosperity" gospel, sometimes called the "health and wealth" gospel.

"Money is the root of all evil."
—THE BIBLE*?*

1 Timothy 6:10 actually says, "The love of money is the root of all evil." Money is just a unit of exchange, and like any other piece of paper, plastic, or rock, it is not evil in and of itself. The opportunity for evil arises, however, when a person is consumed with greed and values the acquisition of things over the duty to love and care for others.

"Money, Come to Me Now!"

I sat on the couch with my arms crossed while the credits rolled, waiting for one of my friends to ask me, "What did you think of the movie?" When they did I replied, "Aside from the subpar acting? I think it had a terrible message."

"What do you mean?" one of them asked, "It's a movie about people becoming Christian. What's so terrible about that?"

"Nothing," I said, "but the movie's message was that if you accept Jesus as your savior then your car will start running again, your wife won't be infertile anymore, and the football team you coach will win the big game. But the Christian life doesn't always work out that way. This movie preached a false prosperity gospel."

The prosperity, or health and wealth, gospel claims that God wants us to always be happy, and if we serve God, then he will bless us with physical and material goods. According to pastor Leroy Thompson in his book *Money Cometh!*:

God wants you to have money, not to be broke and in poverty ... Say this out loud: "Money cometh to me now! God wants me to have plenty of money so I can carry out his covenant. Money cometh to me today, tomorrow, the next day, *every* day. *Money cometh!*"[196]

One of the major tenets of the prosperity gospel is the "law of reciprocity." Basically, if you are generous to other people then other people will be generous to you. The image of a closed or full hand keeping God from blessing people with money, à la our apocryphal Augustine quote, is a favorite among prosperity preachers.

Mega pastor Joel Osteen writes in his book *Your Best Life Now*, "God will not fill a closed fist with good things. Be a giver, rather than a taker ... If you are generous to people in their time of need, God will make sure that other people are generous to you in your time of need."[197] Osteen's wife, Victoria, uses a similar illustration. "You might even be holding on to something good, but good things can also keep our hands too full to embrace God's very best."[198]

The law of reciprocity is very popular among televangelists who encourage their audiences to have "open hands" (and open wallets) to support their ministries. They say God will bless these givers with wealth and happiness because they have kept their "hands open" for the good things God wants to given them.

It's true that God may withhold a blessing until we let go of something that would nullify the value of that blessing, like a possession or relationship we practically idolize. But that does not mean that God always wants to bless us with comfort or wealth. Sometimes God "blesses" us with suffering in order to achieve some greater good, either for ourselves or for other people.

For example, Jacob's son Joseph told his brothers who sold

him into slavery, "You meant evil against me; but God meant it for good, to bring it about that many people should be kept alive" (Gen. 50:20). Jesus said that a man had been born blind not because of anyone's sins, but so that God would be glorified when Christ healed him (John 9:3).

Unlike those who peddle a health and wealth gospel, St. Teresa of Avila said, "We always find that those who walked closest to Christ Our Lord were those who had to bear the greatest trials."[199] These trials can become blessings that help us develop a more intimate relationship with God by turning to him as a source of consolation when everything else fails to provide hope or comfort in our suffering. The book of Sirach gives this advice:

> Accept whatever is brought upon you, and endure it in sorrow; in changes that humble you be patient. For gold and silver are tested in the fire, and acceptable men in the furnace of humiliation. Trust in God, and he will help you; hope in him, and he will make your ways straight. Stay in fear of him, and grow old in him. (Sir. 2:4-6)

Coming Up Empty-Handed

Some people claim Augustine's quote about "full hands" comes from his *City of God*, but I have searched several translations of the work and have not found this quote in any of them. The likelier source is Gerald May's 2007 book, *Addiction and Grace: Love and Spirituality in the Healing of Addictions.* In the first chapter, May says that what sets Christianity apart from other religions is grace, which he says is "a gift that we are free to ignore, reject, ask for, or simply accept . . . We can seek it and try to be open to it, but we cannot control it." He writes:

> Similarly, grace seeks us but will not control us. Saint Augustine once said that God is always trying to give good things

to us, but our hands are too full to receive them. If our hands are full, they are full of things to which we are addicted. And not only our hands, but also our heart, minds, and attention are clogged with addiction. Our addictions fill up the spaces within us, spaces where grace might flow.[200]

May was not citing Augustine in order to show that God will give us wealth if we are generous to others. He was describing how an addict's disordered desire keeps him from receiving God's blessings. He then reminds the reader that addicts can't blame the thing to which they are addicted for their troubles. May even cites this authentic quote from St. John of the Cross: "It is not the things of this world that either occupy the soul or cause it harm, since they enter it not, but rather the will and desire for them."[201]

Even people who are not addicts in the traditional sense, but obsessively chase worldly things like money, sex, relationships, status, or comfort often miss out on the real blessings God wants to give them. Because we were made in the image of God, our souls crave an everlasting joy and infinite goodness that no earthly pleasure can satisfy. We shouldn't keep our "hands empty" for God to give us material goods; we should keep them open so we can receive God himself. St. Augustine realized this after his conversion, and in the opening lines of his *Confessions* he wrote:

Man, who bears about with him his mortality, the witness of his sin, even the witness that you resist the proud, — yet man, this part of your creation, desires to praise you. You move us to delight in praising you; for you have made us for yourself, and our hearts are restless until they rest in you.[202]

> **MISATTRIBUTED**
>
> *"Have patience with all things—*
> *but first with yourself.*
> *Never confuse your mistakes*
> *with your value as a human being.*
> *You are a perfectly valuable, creative,*
> *worthwhile person simply because*
> *you exist. And no amount of triumphs or*
> *tribulations can ever change that."*
> —ST. FRANCIS DE SALES**?**

The first sentence of this quote is fairly close to what St. Francis said, but the rest comes from Michael LeBoeuf's 1982 book *Imagineering*.[203] He wrote, "Accept yourself. St. Francis de Sales wrote, 'Have patience with all things, but first of all yourself.' Never confuse your mistakes with your value as a human being."

LeBoeuf goes on to say the rest of this apocryphal de Sales quote before concluding, "Unconditional self-acceptance is the core of a peaceful mind. And with a peaceful mind, you will have cleared the greatest creative hurdle."[204] Later authors who quoted him simply failed to distinguish LeBoeuf's thoughts from the words he was quoting.

Be Careful What You Pray For?

In 1902 W.W. Jacobs published a short, haunting story called "The Monkey's Paw." It's about a couple named Mr. and Mrs. White, who receive a mummified monkey's paw from a friend in the British Army. The friend tells the couple that the paw grants wishes in horrible ways, but they fail to heed his warning. For example, the couple wishes for two hundred dollars to pay off their mortgage, which comes after their son dies in a workplace accident and his company offers them a "good will" settlement in that exact amount.

I share this macabre story because it is one of the most

famous pieces of literature to contain the theme "Be careful what you wish for."[205] The opposite of the prosperity preachers would be people who say God curses us with sickness and poverty because we have the temerity to ask for health or wealth. This attitude seems to lie behind this quote attributed to St. Teresa of Avila: "There are more tears shed over answered prayers than over unanswered ones."

God might grant a prayer that causes suffering in the short run in order to bring more good in the long run. For example, God might grant a man's request for a job he will later resent with the purpose of showing the man he is called to another career or vocation. But saying people are more likely to suffer when God answers their prayers turns God into a kind of vindictive "monkey's paw," a cruel deity that ironically punishes our sincere requests for help.

But St. Luke tells us that Jesus taught the disciples a parable about a widow who persistently asked a judge for help, in order to teach them "always to pray and not lose heart" (Luke 18:1). In another instance Jesus said, "For everyone who asks receives, and he who seeks finds, and to him who knocks it will be opened" (Luke 11:10).

The earliest citation I can find for this purported St. Teresa quote is in a 1976 interview with author Truman Capote. While talking about his plan to write a variation on the nonfiction novel, he said, "I called the book *Answered Prayers*, which is a quote from [St. Teresa of Avila], who said: 'More tears are shed over answered prayers than unanswered ones.'"[206] In another place Capote admits, "Perhaps that isn't the precise quotation, but we can look it up."[207]

When we look up what St. Teresa wrote we find that she did write about "the gift of tears," but she didn't say God arbitrarily causes us to suffer. In works like *Interior Castle*, St. Teresa taught that prayer is essential to forming an intimate relationship with God. This means that the believer is free to share powerful emotions with God and not merely use prayer as a means to rattle off a litany of requests. She writes, "The tears God gives are now accompanied by joy; however, although they are experienced, there is no striving for them."[208]

The presence of God can be so overwhelming that we can be reduced to tears when we think about our sinfulness and God's inexhaustible love for us in spite of our sins. God is a father so he disciplines us for our good (Heb. 12:10), but he also loves us and desires our good. That's why St. Peter exhorts us to, "Cast all your anxieties on him, for he cares about you" (1 Peter 5:6-7).

We shouldn't think of prayer as the means to get what we want from a God who is nothing more than a cosmic vending machine. James 4:3 even says that sometimes our prayers are not answered because we "ask wrongly," or we care more that "*my* will be done" instead of "*thy* will be done." When we pray we should adore God, repent of sins, and thank him for his blessings and even trials. When we ask, or make supplications, we should do so with the intention of being completely honest with God so that when he says yes we can rejoice and when he says no we can trust that his will is better for us. St. Thérèse of Lisieux put it well: "For me prayer is a surge of the heart, it is a simple look toward Heaven, it is a cry of recognition and of love, embracing both trial and joy."[209]

"He who sings prays twice."
—ST. AUGUSTINE **?**

Paragraph 1156 of the *Catechism* includes this alleged quote and renders the Latin text as "Qui canit bis orat." It says it comes from Augustine's *Enarratio in Psalmum 72*. According to Fr. John Zuhlsdorf, the relevant Latin text says, "He who sings praise, not only sings, but also loves him whom he is singing about/to/for. There is a praise-filled public proclamation in the praise of someone who is confessing/acknowledging (God), in the song of the lover (there is) love."[210] In other words, when a person sings of praises to God this makes God manifest in his song and praise.

The *General Instruction of the Roman Missal* says, "Singing is the sign of the heart's joy" (cf. Acts 2:46). Thus St. Augustine says rightly, "Singing is for one who loves" and there is also an ancient proverb: "Whoever sings well prays twice over."[211] The earliest reference to this quote I have found comes from a 1916 magazine published by the alumni association of St. Francis Seminary. It says, "It is not a mere saw, but an undisputed truth that he who sings well, prays twice."

God's Great Expectations

"The world offers you comfort, but you were not made for comfort, you were made for greatness." At first blush, this quote allegedly from Pope Benedict XVI seems to be a good counterpoint to the prosperity gospel. Our happiness comes not from wealth or material goods, but from something greater that God can offer us. But this quote is also problematic because we must ask, "God made me for greatness . . . in what?"

Most of the people the world considers "great" aren't saints but athletes, movie stars, and billionaires. Is that the kind of greatness God wants for me? Am I supposed to be "great" at being Catholic? The saints would never say they were "great" at being holy. According to St. John of the Cross, "To be taken with love for a soul, God does not look on its greatness, but the greatness of its humility."[212] Pope Benedict did believe we were made for "greatness," and in his address to a group of German pilgrims he explains exactly what that means:

The ways of the Lord are not easy, but we were not created for an easy life, but for *great things*, for *goodness* . . . Christ did not promise an easy life. Those who desire comforts have dialed the wrong number. Rather, he shows us the way to *great things*, the good, toward an authentic human life [emphasis added].[213]

We were made for greatness in the sense of belonging to that which is greatness itself. In his encyclical *Spe Salvi*, Pope Benedict wrote, "Man was created for greatness—for God himself; he was created to be filled by God. But his heart is too small for the greatness to which it is destined. It must be stretched."[214] In other words, if we cling to the comforts of this world for which we were not made, then our hearts will never be big enough to receive the greatness of God for which we were made.

A Better Quote

> **"You wish to be great, begin from the least. You are thinking to construct some mighty fabric in height; first think of the foundation of humility."**
> —ST. AUGUSTINE[215]

Throughout Scripture God constantly upends our human expectations. Israel is selected to be the chosen people even though other nations were older and mightier in stature and power. Younger sons are often chosen to be the mediators of covenants when older sons would usually have been the first to receive such an honor. God routinely uses the small, weak, and humble to display his grand, magnificent power.

If we want to serve God, then we must focus on how small we are in relation to him and be willing to let God work through our actions, for whatever purpose he may have. John the Baptist was sent so that he could prepare the people to receive the Messiah, something we are all still called to do as we "prepare the way" for people to come to know Jesus Christ. But rather than consider himself a mighty servant of God he said of Jesus, "He must increase, but I must decrease" (John 3:30).

The same is true for us: we must always die to self and decrease in pride so that God can increase within us and provide us with life-giving grace to save our souls and be witnesses of his salvation to the whole world.

What the Saints DID Say

THE FOLLOWING IS not an exhaustive collection of sayings from important figures in Catholic history, but it is a good sample portfolio of the wisdom with which God has blessed the Church through the men and women who have served him.

St. Augustine

✛ "Too late did I love you, O Fairness, so ancient, and yet so new! Too late did I love you!" —*Confessions*

✛ "You have formed us for yourself, and our hearts are restless till they find rest in You." —*Confessions*

✛ "The confession of evil works is the first beginning of good works." —*Tractates on the Gospel of John*

✛ "Patience is companion of wisdom, not handmaid of concupiscence: patience is the friend of a good conscience, not the foe of innocence." —*On Patience*

✛ "For even in the likeness of the sufferings, there remains an unlikeness in the sufferers; and though exposed to the same anguish, virtue and vice are not the same thing." —*City of God*

✛ "You wish to be great, begin from the least. You are thinking to construct some mighty fabric in height; first think of the foundation of humility." —Sermon 19 on the New Testament

St. Bernard of Clairvaux

✣ "We are to love God for himself because of a twofold reason: Nothing is more reasonable; nothing more profitable." —*On Loving God*

✣ "For who is free from defects? He lacks everything who thinks he lacks nothing." —*On Consideration*

✣ "No misery is more genuine than false joy." —*On Consideration*

G.K. Chesterton

✣ "The great painter boasted that he mixed all his colors with brains, and the great saint may be said to mix all his thoughts with thanks. All goods look better when they look like gifts." —*Saint Francis of Assisi*

✣ "The difficulty of explaining, 'why I am a Catholic' is that there are ten thousand reasons all amounting to one reason: that Catholicism is true." —"Why I Am a Catholic"

✣ "A Catholic is a person who has plucked up courage to face the incredible and inconceivable idea that something else may be wiser than he is." —"The Surrender Upon Sex"

✣ "We do not really want a religion that is right where we are right. What we want is a religion that is right where we are wrong." —*The Catholic Church and Conversion*

✣ "It is not bigotry to be certain we are right; but it is bigotry to be unable to imagine how we might possibly have gone wrong." —*The Catholic Church and Conversion*

✛ "Religious liberty might be supposed to mean that every-body is free to discuss religion. In practice it means that hardly anybody is allowed to mention it." —*Autobiography*

Pope St. Clement I

✛ "By him we look up to the heights of heaven. By him we behold, as in a glass, his immaculate and most excellent vis-age." —*1 Clement*

✛ "Cleave to the holy [saints], for those that cleave to them shall [themselves] be made holy [saints]." —*1 Clement*

✛ "[The Apostles] appointed those [ministers] already men-tioned, and afterward gave instructions, that when these should fall asleep, other approved men should succeed them in their ministry." —*1 Clement*

St. Cyprian of Carthage

✛ "He can no longer have God for his Father, who has not the Church for his mother." —*Treatise 1*

✛ "How can you ask to be heard of God, when you yourself do not hear yourself?" —*Treatise 4*

✛ "To him who still remains in this world no repentance is too late." —*Treatise 5*

St. Elizabeth Ann Seton

✛ "We must often draw the comparison between time and eternity. This is the remedy of all our troubles. How small will the present moment appear when we enter that great ocean!" —*Life of Mrs. Eliza A. Seton*

✛ "The most tender Father of all; my immense God; I his atom." —*Life of Mrs. Eliza A. Seton*

✛ "You may sow here indeed in tears, but you may be sure there to reap in joy." —*Life of Mrs. Eliza A. Seton*

✛ "Young people especially should fight cheerfully, since our Lord has so kindly called you in the morning of your days, and not exposed you to the anguish and remorse we feel after so many years of sin." —*Life of Mrs. Eliza A. Seton*

St. Francis of Assisi

✛ "Even the demons did not crucify him, but you together with them crucified him and still crucify him by taking delight in vices and sins." —*Admonitions*

✛ "All this reverence which is paid to me I never take to myself, but simply pass it all on to God." —*The Wisdom of St. Francis and his Companions*

✛ "What are the servants of God if not his minstrels, who must move people's hearts and lift them up to spiritual joy?" —*The Mirror of Perfection*

St. Francis de Sales

✛ "In our Lord's passion love and death blend so inextricably that no heart can contain one without the other." —*Introduction to the Devout Life & Treatise on the Love of God*

✛ "Have patience with everyone, but especially with yourself." —*The Spirit of Saint Francis de Sales*

✛ "Always be as indulgent as you can, remembering that one can catch more flies with a spoonful of honey than with a hundred barrels of vinegar. If you must exceed on one or the other side, let it be on that of indulgence." —*The Spirit of Saint Francis de Sales*

Pope St. Gregory the Great

✚ "Practice should be sustained by prayer, and prayer by practice." —*Moralia*

✚ "[The Word of God] is, as it were, a kind of river, if I may so liken it, which is both shallow and deep, wherein both the lamb may find a footing, and the elephant float at large." —*Moralia*

✚ "Merely to love things above is already to mount on high." —*Moralia*

St. Josemaría Escrivá

✚ "Don't forget that the saint is not the person who never falls, but rather the one who never fails to get up again, humbly and with a holy stubbornness." —*Friends of God*

✚ "With God's grace, you have to tackle and carry out the impossible, because anybody can do what is possible." —*The Forge*

✚ "The higher a statue is raised, the harder and more dangerous the impact when it falls." —*Furrow*

St. Ignatius of Antioch

✚ "It is not that I want merely to be called a Christian, but to actually be one. Yes, if I prove to be one, then I can have the name." —Epistle to the Romans

✛ "It is better for a man to be silent and be [a Christian], than to talk and not to be one. It is good to teach, if he who speaks also acts." —Epistle to the Ephesians

✛ "Wherever the bishop shall appear, there let the multitude [of the people] also be; even as, wherever Jesus Christ is, there is the Catholic Church." —Epistle to the Smyrnaeans

St. Jerome
✛ "In the lives of Christians we look not to the beginnings but to the endings." —Letter 54

✛ "A friend is long sought, hardly found, and with difficulty kept." —Letter 3

✛ "Do not let your deeds belie your words; lest when you speak in church someone may mentally reply, 'Why do you not practice what you profess?'" —Letter 52

St. John of the Cross
✛ "My spirit has become dry because it forgets to feed on you." —*The Collected Works of Saint John of the Cross*

✛ "To be taken with love for a soul, God does not look on its greatness, but the greatness of its humility." —*The Collected Works of St. John of the Cross*

✛ "It is not the things of this world that either occupy the soul or cause it harm, since they enter it not, but rather the will and desire for them." —*Ascent of Mount Carmel*

Blessed John Henry Newman
✛ "To be deep in history is to cease to be Protestant." —*An Essay on the Development of Christian Doctrine*

✛ "In a higher world it is otherwise, but here below to live is to change, and to be perfect is to have changed often." —*An Essay on the Development of Christian Doctrine*

✛ "Nothing would be done at all, if a man waited till he could do it so well that no one could find fault with it." —*Lectures on the Present Position of Catholics in England*

Pope St. John Paul II

✛ "Be not afraid! Open wide the doors to Christ!" —Homily for the Inauguration of His Pontificate, St. Peter's Square, Sunday, October 22, 1978

✛ "The gospel lives in conversation with the culture, and if the Church holds back from the culture, the gospel itself falls silent." —The Plenary Meeting of the Pontifical Council for Social Communications, March 1, 2002

✛ "It is Christ you seek when you dream of happiness." —Fifteenth World Youth Day Address, August 19, 2000

✛ "We are not the sum of our weaknesses and failures. We are the sum of the Father's love for us." —Seventeenth World Youth Day Solemn Mass, July 28, 2002

✛ "As the family goes, so goes the nation and so goes the whole world in which we live." —Homily, Perth, November, 30 1986

✛ "Freedom consists not in doing what we like, but in having the right to do what we ought." —Homily, Baltimore, October 8, 1995

Venerable Fulton Sheen

✛ "There are not a hundred people in America who hate the Catholic Church. There are millions of people who hate what they wrongly believe to be the Catholic Church—which is, of course, quite a different thing." —Foreword, *Radio Replies*

✛ "Right is right if nobody is right, and wrong is wrong if everybody is wrong." —*God's World and Our Place in It*

St. Teresa of Avila

✛ "Those who in fact risk all for God will find that they have both lost all and gained all. I don't say that I'm like this, but I wish I were." —*The Book of Her Life*

✛ "We must all try to be preachers by our deeds." —*The Way of Perfection*

✛ "It will be the fault of ignorance, not malice, if I say anything contrary to the doctrine of the Holy Roman Catholic Church." —*Interior Castle*

✛ "I believe we shall never learn to know ourselves except by endeavoring to know God, for, beholding his greatness we are struck by our own baseness, his purity shows our foulness, and by meditating on his humility we find how very far we are from being humble." —*Interior Castle*

✛ "We always find that those who walked closest to Christ Our Lord were those who had to bear the greatest trials." —*Interior Castle*

St. Teresa of Calcutta (Mother Teresa)

✟ "The fruit of prayer is love. The fruit of love is service. Only when you pray can you really serve the poor." —*Mother Teresa of Calcutta: A Personal Portrait*

✟ "Love is the ultimate gift of ourselves to others." —*Where There Is Love, There Is God: Her Path to Closer Union with God and Greater Love for Others*

✟ "By blood, I am Albanian. By citizenship, an Indian. By faith, I am a Catholic nun. As to my calling, I belong to the world. As to my heart, I belong entirely to the Heart of Jesus." —*Just Spirituality: How Faith Practices Fuel Social Action*

St. Thérèse of Lisieux

✟ "You cannot be half a saint. You must be a whole saint or no saint at all." —*Two Letters of St. Thérèse of Lisieux to Abbé Bellière*

✟ "My vocation is love." —*The Story of a Soul*

✟ "Perfection consists in doing his will, in being that which he wants us to be." —*The Story of a Soul*

St. Thomas Aquinas

✟ "To love God is something greater than to know him." —*Summa Theologiae*

✟ "Charity, by which God and neighbor are loved, is the most perfect friendship." —*On Charity*

✟ "Whatever we do or suffer for a friend is pleasant, because love is the principal cause of pleasure." —*Summa Theologiae*

✠ "Now pain or sorrow for that which is truly evil cannot be the greatest evil: for there is something worse, namely, either not to reckon as evil that which is really evil, or not to reject it." —*Summa Theologiae*

Notes

Acknowledgments

1 John Henry Newman, *Lectures on the Present Position of Catholics in England* (London: Longmans, Green, and Co, 1908) 403. A similar sentiment can be found in the Chesterton quip "If something is worth doing, it's worth doing badly," G.K. Chesterton, "Folly and Female Education," in *What's Wrong with the World?* (1910; n.p.: Pantianos Classics, 201), 121. Keep in mind this quote is often taken out of context. Chesterton did not mean that any venture is worth doing in a haphazard way. Rather, he was talking about how the important parts of our everyday lives are worth doing ourselves, apart from having "professionals" do them, even if the quality isn't as good. For example, learning to cook or play a musical instrument is a worthwhile pursuit even if the end product, at least at first, is "bad" when compared to what a professional can do. Chesterton was specifically referring to the goodness of women devoting themselves to full-time childcare and maintaining "the prime truth about woman" instead of shuffling their children off to be raised by "professionals" in day care. Concerning this present work, even though in one sense I am a professional writer, I am not a professional historian or archivist. Still, I believe this book is worth writing even if a later reader proves me wrong about certain quotes I have investigated.

Introduction

2 "'Beam me up, Scotty!' was never actually uttered by any Star Trek character. 'Beam us up, Mr. Scott!' was in the 1968 *Gamesters of Triskelion*." Maria Konnikova, "'Beam Us Up, Mr. Scott!': Why Misquotations Catch On," *Atlantic,* August 15, 2012, www.theatlantic.com/ entertainment/archive/2012/08/beam-us-up-mr-scott-why-misquotations-catch-on/261146/.

3 The apocryphal story about Washington and the cherry tree first appeared in Mason Locke Weem's biography about Washington. Edward G. Lengel, *Inventing George Washington: America's Founder, in Myth and Memory* (New York: Harper Collins, 2011), 21-22. The Einstein quote

actually comes from Rita Mae Brown's novel *Sudden Death,* where it is attributed to the fictional Jane Fulton. Brown, *Sudden Death* (New York: Bantam Books, 1983), 68. UCLA Bruins coach Red Sanders originated the saying that winning is "the only thing," but Lombardi heard it and probably repeated it on occasion. David Maraniss, *When Pride Still Mattered: A Life of Vince Lombardi* (New York: Simon & Schuster, 1999), 369.

4 *The Complete Works St. Teresa of Jesus,* trans., E. Allison Peers, vol. 3 (New York: Burns and Oates, 2002), 256.

5 Hesketh Pearson, *Oscar Wilde: His Life and Wit* (New York: Harper & Brothers, 1946), 323. Cited in "Lovers: They Sing a Song Only You Can Hear," QuoteInvestigator.com, December 1, 2015, quoteinvestigator.com/2015/12/01/lovers/#return-note-12568-4.

6 A.H. Saxon, *P.T. Barnum: The Legend and the Man* (New York: Columbia University Press, 1989), 335.

7 Ibid., 336-37.

8 Niraj Chokshi, "That Wasn't Mark Twain: How a Misquotation Is Born" *New York Times,* April 26, 2017, www.nytimes.com/2017/04/26/books/famous-misquotations.html?mcubz=1.

9 *1 Clement 46.*

Chapter 1

10 Mark Galli, "Speak the Gospel," *Christianity Today,* May 21, 2009, www.christianitytoday.com/ct/2009/mayweb-only/120-42.0.html.

11 Daisy Osborn, *Woman without Limits* (Tulsa, OK: Osfo Publishers, 1990), 245.

12 Pat McCloskey, OFM, "Where Did Saint Francis Say That?," www.franciscanmedia.org/origin-of-saint-francis-peace-prayer/.

13 Gary Krause, *God's Great Missionaries* (Nampa, ID: Pacific Press Publishing, 2008), 36.

14 Mother Teresa, *Love: A Fruit Always in Season* (San Francisco: Ignatius Press, 1987), 108.

15 *Senate Daily Journal,* Legislature of the State of California, May 10, 1972, 2182.

16 *The Epistle of Mathetes to Diognetus*, 5.

17 Julian the Apostate, *Letter to Arsacius*.

18 *Butler's Lives of the Saints*, vol. 4 (Collegeville, MN: The Liturgical Press, 1999), 106.

19 Jerome Lawrence and Robert E. Lee, *Inherit the Wind* (New York: Dramatist Play Service, 2000), 43.

20 *Summa Theologiae* I.113.4, cited in Father Horton, "St. Thomas and the Means of Conversion," Fauxtations.wordpress.com, August 12, 2015, fauxtations.wordpress.com/2015/08/12/st-thomas-and-the-means-of-conversion/.

21 Thomas of Celano, "The Legend of Three Companions," in *Francis of Assisi: Early Documents,* vol. 2 (St. Bonaventure, NY: Franciscan Institute of St. Bonaventure University, 2000), 84.

22 James C. Howell, *Conversations with St. Francis* (Nashville, TN: Abingdon Press, 2008), 78.

23 Augustine Thompson, *Francis of Assisi: A New Biography* (Ithaca, NY: Cornell University Press, 2012), 51.

24 Mark Galli, "Speak the Gospel," *Christianity Today*, May 21, 2009, www.christianitytoday.com/ct/2009/mayweb-only/120-42.0.html.

25 "A Mirror of the Perfection" *Francis of Assisi: Early Documents,* vol. 3 (St. Bonaventure, NY: Franciscan Institute of St. Bonaventure University, 2001), 348.

26 Thomas of Celano, *The Lives of St. Francis of Assisi,* trans., A.G. Ferrers Howell (London: Methuen & Co., 1926), 295.

27 *The Little Flowers of St. Francis of Assisi,* ed., H.E. Manning (London: Burns and Lambert, 1864), 82. The text is anonymous but scholars generally agree that Brunforte is the author.

28 Francis of Assisi, "Fragments," in *Francis of Assisi: Early Documents,* vol. 1 (St. Bonaventure, NY: Franciscan Institute of St. Bonaventure University, 2000), 91.

29 Teresa of Avila, *The Way of Perfection,* trans., E. Allison Peers (New York: Doubleday, 1991), 263.

30 Joseph Esper, *Saintly Solutions to Life's Common Problems* (Manchester, NH: Sophia Institute Press, 2001), 182, cited in Father Horton, "St. Teresa of Ávila on Your Past and the Devil's Future," Fauxtations. wordpress.com, March 16, 2015, fauxtations.wordpress.com/ 2015/03/16/st-teresa-of-avila-on-your-past-and-the-devils-future/.

31 Francis of Assisi, "Later Admonition and Exhortation," in *Francis of Assisi: Early Documents,* vol. 1 (St. Bonaventure, NY: Franciscan Institute of St. Bonaventure University, 2000), 49.

32 Francis of Assisi, "The Undated Writings" in *Francis of Assisi: Early Documents,* vol. 1 (St. Bonaventure, NY: Franciscan Institute of St. Bonaventure University, 2000), 137.

33 Francis of Assisi, "The Earlier Rule," in *Francis of Assisi: Early Documents,* vol. 1 (St. Bonaventure, NY: Franciscan Institute of St. Bonaventure University, 2000), 75.

34 Teresa of Avila, *The Way of Perfection* trans., E. Allison Peers (New York: Image Books, 1991) 95.

35 *Letter 52*

Chapter 2

36 Mother Teresa, "Whatever You Did unto One of the Least, You Did unto Me," address at the National Prayer Breakfast, February 3, 1994, www.ewtn.com/library/issues/prbkmter.txt.

37 Susan Jacoby, *The Great Agnostic: Robert Ingersoll and American*

Freethought (New Haven, CT: Yale University Press, 2013), Kindle edition.

38 Robert Ingersoll, "The Children of the Stage" in *Ingersoll's Greatest Lectures* (New York: The Freethought Press Association, 1944), 56.

39 Kimberly Yao, "Who Gives? The Determinants of Charitable Giving, Volunteering, and Their Relationship," *Wharton Research Scholars* (May 2015), 13.

40 Fr. Leo Maasburg, *Mother Teresa of Calcutta: A Personal Portrait* (San Francisco: Ignatius Press, 2011), 80.

41 "Mother Teresa and Communion in the Hand Question from Roberto Lionello on 01-13-2005," www.ewtn.com/v/experts/showmessage_print.asp?number=425165&language=en.

42 Mother Teresa, "Whatever You Did unto One of the Least, You Did unto Me," address at the National Prayer Breakfast, February 3, 1994, www.ewtn.com/library/issues/prbkmter.txt.

43 Ibid.

44 "Mother Teresa: On receiving Holy Communion in the Hand," www.motherteresa.org/08_info/receivingc.html.

45 Fr. George W. Rutler, "On the Canonization of Saint Teresa of Calcutta," *Crisis,* August 24, 2016, www.crisismagazine.com/2016/memories-mother-canonization-saint-teresa-calcutta.

46 *Redemptionis Sacramentum*, 92.

47 *Catechetical Lecture* 23, 21.

48 Kent M. Keith, *Anyway: The Paradoxical Commandments: Finding Personal Meaning in a Crazy World* (New York: G.P. Putnam's Sons, 2001), 5.

49 Robert Heinlein, *Stranger in a Strange Land* (New York: G.P. Putnam's Sons, 1987), 363.

50 Mother Teresa, *Where There Is Love, There Is God: Her Path to Closer Union with God and Greater Love for Others,* ed., Brian Kolodiejchuk (New York: Random House, 2010), 26.

51 Mother Teresa, *A Simple Path* (New York: Random House, 1995), 185.

52 Keith, *Anyway: The Paradoxical Commandments,* 5.

53 "The Mother Teresa Connection," www.paradoxicalcommandments. com/mother-teresa-connection.html.

54 Mother Teresa, Nobel Lecture, December 11, 1979, www.nobelprize. org/nobel_prizes/peace/laureates/1979/teresa-lecture.html.

55 Mother Teresa, *Mother Teresa: Come Be My Light: The Private Writings of the Saint of Calcutta,* ed., Brian Kolodiejchuk (New York: Doubleday, 2007), 307.

56 Mae Elise Cannon, *Just Spirituality: How Faith Practices Fuel Social Action* (Downers Grove, IL: InterVarsity Press, 2013), 19.

57 St. Francis de Sales, *Introduction to the Devout Life,* ed., Allan Ross (Mineola, NY: Dover Publications Inc, 2009), 38-39.

Chapter 3

58 "For years I've been stressing with regard to UFOs that extraordinary claims require extraordinary evidence. The evidence for life on Mars is not yet extraordinary enough." Carl Sagan, *Billions & Billions: Thoughts on Life and Death at the Brink of the Millennium* (New York: Ballantine, 1997), 60.

59 "AP FACT CHECK: Pope isn't seeking Islam, Christianity merger," *Associated Press,* January 02, 2017, www.apnews.com/dce69af-02893466e88c91d41292cbbcc.

60 Dan Evon "Religious Replicates," *Snopes.com* September 24, 2015, www.snopes.com/religious-replicates/.

61 "Pope at Mass: Culture of Encounter Is the Foundation of Peace," *Vatican Radio,* May 22, 2013, en.radiovaticana.va/storico/2013/05/22/

pope_at_mass_culture_of_encounter_is_the_foundation_of_peace/
en1-694445.

62 Thomas Rosica, "Explanatory Note on the Meaning of 'Salvation' in
Francis' Daily Homily of May 22," May 23, 2013, zenit.org/articles/
explanatory-note-on-the-meaning-of-salvation-in-francis-daily-
homily-of-may-22/.

63 Subtropic Productions LLC, "An atheist is a man who has no invisible means of support," December 14, 2014, www.thisdayinquotes.
com/2011/12/atheist-is-man-who-has-no-invisible.html.

64 Harry Emerson Fosdick. *On Being a Real Person* (New York: Harper-
Collins, 1943), 250.

65 Sermo 15, *De passione Domine*, 3-4: PL 54, 366-67. Cited in Fr. Devin
Roza, *Fulfilled in Christ: The Sacraments. A Guide to Symbols and Types
in the Bible and Tradition* (Steubenville, OH: Emmaus Academic,
2015), 39. A different translation can be found in "Sermon 66" in *Leo
the Great: Sermons,* trans., Jane Patricia Freeland and Agnes Josephine
Conway (Washington DC: Catholic University of America Press,
1996), 288-89.

66 Wendy Wright, *Francis de Sales: Introduction to the Devout Life & Treatise
on the Love of God* (Stella Niagara, NY: De Sales Resource Center,
1993), 160.

67 Bruce Marshall, *The World, The Flesh, and Father Smith* (New York:
Houghton Mifflin, 1945), 108.

68 Rosica, "Explanatory Note on the Meaning of 'Salvation.'"

69 Pope Francis, "Audience with the Diplomatic Corps Accredited to
the Holy See," March 22, 2013, w2.vatican.va/content/francesco/en/
speeches/2013/march/documents/papa-francesco_20130322_cor-
po-diplomatico.html.

70 *Nostra Aetate*, 2.

71 Neil Gaiman, *Tumblr,* February 12, 2013, neil-gaiman.tumblr.com/

post/42909304300/my-moms-a-librarian-and-planning-to-put-lit-erary.

72 G.K. Chesterton, *Tremendous Trifles* (London: Meuthen & Co., 1909), 102.

73 See also Fr. William Most, "Tragic Errors of Leonard Feeney," www.ewtn.com/library/scriptur/feeney.txt.

74 Fourth Lateran Council, canon 1, sourcebooks.fordham.edu/halsall/basis/lateran4.asp.

75 Department of Public Welfare of the State of Vermont, "Biennial Report," June 30, 1936, 116. A portion of the document can be viewed at https://books.google.com/books?id=jsvoAAAAIAAJ&dq&focus=-searchwithinvolume&q=Persians

76 This is, of course, barring some of the fanciful and incorrect historical claims of Mormonism. For more on that subject see my booklet *20 Answers: Mormonism*, published by Catholic Answers Press.

77 *Lumen Gentium*, 16.

78 G.K. Chesterton "Where All Roads Lead," in *The Collected Works of G. K. Chesterton,* vol. 3 (1922; reprint San Francisco: Ignatius Press, 1990), 38. Special thanks to Paul Nowak, "The Seven Most Popular G.K. Chesterton Quotes He Never Said," *The Federalist,* May 6, 2014, thefederalist.com/2014/05/06/the-seven-most-popular-g-k-chester-ton-quotes-he-never-said/.

79 Ibid., 37.

80 Originally from Trent Horn, *Why We're Catholic: Our Reasons for Faith, Hope, and Love* (El Cajon: Catholic Answers Press, 2017), 339.

81 *Lumen Gentium*, 16.

Chapter 4

82 Fr. Barton T. Geger, "Myths, Misquotes and Misconceptions about St. Ignatius Loyola," *Jesuit Higher Education: A Journal* 5, no. 1 (May

2016): 12. Fr. Geger mentions this in a footnote: "The poems have not survived. On Ignatius's early religiosity see Pedro de Leturia, S.J., *Iñigo de Loyola,* trans., Aloysius J. Owen (New York: Le Moyne College Press, 1949), 27-53, and Paul Dudon, S.J., *St. Ignatius of Loyola,* trans., William J. Young, S.J. (Milwaukee: Bruce Publishing, 1953), 17-24."

83 Ibid.

84 James Brodrick, *Saint Ignatius Loyola: The Pilgrim Years, 1491-1538* (San Francisco: Ignatius Press, 1998), 77.

85 Avery Dulles, "What Distinguishes the Jesuits?," *America: The Jesuit Review* 196, no. 2 (January 15, 2007), www.americamagazine.org/faith/2007/01/15/what-distinguishes-jesuits.

86 Laurie Goodstein, "Serenity Prayer Skeptic Now Credits Niebuhr," *New York Times,* November 28, 2009, query.nytimes.com/gst/fullpage.html?res=9903E4D71531F93BA15752C1A96F9C8B63.

87 When asked if the prayer was original to him Niebuhr said he thought it was, but admitted, "It may have been spooking around for centuries." Nell Wing, *Grateful to Have Been There: My 42 Years with Bill And Lois, and the Evolution of Alcoholics Anonymous,* 2nd ed. (Center City, MN: Hazeldon, 1998), 180.

88 "'Pray as if everything depended on God and work as if everything depended on you.' Even when we have done our work, the food we receive is still a gift from our Father; it is good to ask him for it and to thank him, as Christian families do when saying grace at meals."

89 Joseph Cardinal Ratzinger and Christoph Schönborn, *Introduction to the Catechism of the Catholic Church* (San Francisco: Ignatius Press, 1994), 26.

90 Cardinal Joseph Ratzinger, "Worthiness to Receive Holy Communion: General Principles" *Memorandum sent by Cardinal Ratzinger to Cardinal McCarrick* July, 2004, www.ewtn.com/library/curia/cdfworthycom.htm.

91 Joseph Guibert, *The Jesuits: Their Spiritual Doctrine and Practice*, trans., William J. Young, ed., George E. Ganss (Chicago: Loyola University Press, 1964), 148.

92 *De ratione in gubernando* 6.14, cited in ibid., 148.

93 Father Horton, "St. Francis and Doing the Impossible," Fauxtations.wordpress.com, February 10, 2015, fauxtations.wordpress.com/2015/02/10/st-francis-and-doing-the-impossible/.

94 Josemaría Escrivá, "The Forge, 216," in *The Way/Furrow/The Forge* (Scepter Publishers, New York, 2001), 620.

95 Crayon Blanc, "Don't Be Contented!," *American Phrenological Journal* 47 (January 1868), 27.

96 W.T.K., "A Few Things about Preaching and Prayer" *Evangelical Repository* 1, no. 4 (June 1867), 277.

97 *Thoughts of St. Ignatius Loyola for Every Day of the Year From the Scintillae Ignatianae compiled by Gabriel Hevenesi, S.J.* trans. Alan G. McDougall (New York: Fordham University Press, 2006) 15.

98 J.P.M. Walsh, "'Work As if Everything Depends On—Who?,'" *The Way Supplement* 70 (Spring 1991), 125.

99 *Laborem Exercens*, 27.

100 Walsh, "'Work As If Everything Depends On—Who?'" 128.

101 Augustine Thompson, *Francis of Assisi: A New Biography* (Ithaca, NY: Cornell University Press, 2012), ix.

102 Christian Renoux, "The Origin of the Peace Prayer of St. Francis," *Franciscan Archive,* www.franciscan-archive.org/franciscana/peace.html.

103 This is an adaption from the following reference: "Blessed is he who loveth and doth not therefore desire to be loved; blessed is he who feareth and doth not therefore desire to be feared; blessed is he who

serveth and doth not therefore desire to be served; blessed is he who
behaveth well toward others and doth not desire that others behave
well toward him; and because these are great things the foolish do
not rise to them." Fr. Paschal Robinson, *The Golden Sayings of Blessed Brother Giles of Assisi* (Philadelphia: Dolphin Press, 1907), 5.

104 Catherine of Siena, "To Stefano Maconi." in *St. Catherine of Siena
As Seen in Her Letters,* trans., Vida Dutton Scudder (New York: E.P.
Dutton, 1905), 305.

105 Timothy Phillips, "Whose Hands? Another Possible Case of Cumu-
lative Authorship," November 7, 2011, mimuspolyglottos.blogspot.
com/2011/11/whose-hands-another-possible-case-of.html.

106 Mark Guy Pearse, "January 3, 1888, address," *Evangelical Christendom*
42, February 1, 1888, 46.

107 "Sarah Eliza Rowntree gave an interesting account of the recent
establishment of the "Home" in Pearl Street, and the progress of the
Mission there. She appealed for more workers to assist its further
usefulness, concluding with some words of Mark Guy Pearse, 'Remember Christ has no human body now upon the earth but yours
. . . ,'" "The Bedford Institute First Day School and Home Mission
Association," *The British Friend* 1, no. 1 (January 1, 1892): 15.

108 "Maxims for Her Nuns," in *Complete Works St. Teresa of Avila,* trans.,
E. Allison Peers, vol. 3 (New York: Burns and Oates, 2002), 257.

Chapter 5
109 "Leno Bible," www.youtube.com/watch?v=nAZevVS-oKU.

110 George Barna, *The Second Coming of the Church* (Nashville, TN:
Thomas Nelson, 1998), 22.

111 Euripides, Fragment 435, cited in John Bartlett, *Bartlett's Familiar
Quotations,* ed., Geoffrey O'Brien, 18th ed. (New York: Little,
Brown, 2012), 59.

112 Sophocles, Fragment 288, cited in ibid. 59.

113 William J. Bennett, *The Book of Virtues for Young People: A Treasury of Great Moral Stories* (New York: Simon and Schuster, 1997), 144.

114 Algernon Sidney, *Discourses On Government,* vol. II (New York: Deare and Andrews, 1805), 214.

115 Barna, *The Second Coming of the Church,* 22.

116 William Cowper, "Light Shining out of Darkness," Hymn 68, *Olney Hymns,* 1779.

117 Fr. M. Raphael Simon, *The Glory of Thy People: The Story of a Conversion* (New York: Macmillan, 1949), xiii.

118 *Complete Works St. Teresa of Avila,* trans., E. Allison Peers, vol. 3 (New York: Burns and Oates, 2002), 288.

119 Council of Trent, Session 6, 8.

120 Richard B. Gaffin, Jr., "Justification in Luke-Acts," in *Right with God: Justification in the Bible and the World,* ed., D.A. Carson (Eugene, OR: Wipf and Stock, 2002), 124.

Chapter 6

121 "A New Strategy. An Ambitious Project," *Alfa y Omega,* interview with Archbishop Vincenzo Paglia, www.vincenzopaglia.it/index.php/a-new-strategy-an-ambitious-project.html.

122 See also Todd Aglialoro, "Does the Truth Need Our Help?," *Catholic Answers Magazine,* July 24, 2017, www.catholic.com/magazine/online-edition/does-the-truth-need-our-help.

123 "All of St. Augustine's works are available in Latin online. I searched for *leo* (all forms of the word for lion), and *verita* (all forms of the word for truth). They occur in the same document 125 times, but never close enough even to be the inspiration for this quotation." Father Horton, "St. Augustine: The Truth Is Like a Lion," Fauxtations.wordpress.com, October 18, 2015, fauxtations.wordpress.com/2015/10/18/st-augustine-the-truth-is-like-a-lion/.

124 C.H. Spurgeon, "The Lover of God's Law Filled with Peace," *Metropolitan Tabernacle*, Newington [London], January 22, 1888, www.ccel.org/ccel/spurgeon/sermons34.iii.html.

125 "The Bible (Part Second)," from a speech given at the British and Foreign Bible Society on May 5, 1875, in *Speeches by C.H. Spurgeon at Home and Abroad,* ed., G.H. Pike (London: Passmore & Alabaster, 1878), 17.

126 *Contra Faustum*, XVII.

127 *The First Apology*, 12.

128 *City of God*, Book XVI, 2.

129 Christopher Rengers, OFM, and Matthew E. Bunson, *The 35 Doctors of the Church* (Charlotte, NC: TAN Books, 2014), 344.

130 *Summa Theologiae*, I.II 2.5

131 *Summa Theologiae*, II.II 1.5

132 Ibid.

133 Ibid.

134 De Praedest. sanct. 2.5, cited in Avery Cardinal Dulles, *A History of Apologetics* (San Francisco, Ignatius Press, 2005), 77.

Chapter 7

135 Richard Dawkins, *A Devil's Chaplain* (New York: Houghton Mifflin Harcourt, 2003), 139.

136 George Alexander Kennedy, *The Cambridge History of Literary Criticism*, vol. 1 (Cambridge: Cambridge University Press, 1989), 337.

137 *On the Flesh of Christ*, 3.

138 *Prescription Against Heretics*, 7.

139 Kennedy, *The Cambridge History of Literary Criticism*, vol. 1, 337.

140 St. Augustine, *City of God,* 22.17.

141 St. Augustine, *Of the Good of Widowhood,* 2.

142 Pliny the Elder, *The Natural History,* chap. 64, "Of the Form of the Earth."

143 David C. Lindberg and Ronald L. Numbers, "Beyond War and Peace: A Reappraisal of the Encounter between Christianity and Science," *Church History* 55, no. 3 (1986): 342.

144 Robert G. Ingersoll, "Individuality" (1873). Available online at https://infidels.org/library/historical/robert_ingersoll/individuality.html.

145 Maurice A. Finocchiaro, *Retrying Galileo, 1633–1992* (Los Angeles: University of California Press, 2007), 114.

146 The detail about Galileo being placed under house arrest is found in the Tuscan ambassador's letters of February 13 and April 16, 1633, to the king of Tuscany.

147 Pope John Paul II, *L'Osservatore Romano,* November 4, 1992.

148 James Hannam, "Science Versus Christianity?," Patheos.com, May 18, 2010, http://www.patheos.com/resources/additional-resources/2010/05/science-versus-christianity.

149 First Vatican Council documents "Canons: 2. On revelation," available online at www.ewtn.com/library/councils/v1.htm#5.

150 According to the *Catechism,* "The Trinity is a mystery of faith in the strict sense, one of the mysteries that are hidden in God, which can never be known unless they are revealed by God. To be sure, God has left traces of his trinitarian being in his work of creation and in his revelation throughout the Old Testament. But his inmost Being as Holy Trinity is a mystery that is inaccessible to reason alone or even to Israel's faith before the Incarnation of God's Son and the

sending of the Holy Spirit" (237).

151 Dawkins, *A Devil's Chaplain*, 139.

152 See, for example, St. Augustine's *De Trinitate* (*On the Trinity*), question thirty-one of the first part of St. Thomas's *Summa Theologiae*, and Cardinal Joseph Ratzinger's discussion of the triune God in his *Introduction to Christianity*.

153 G.K. Chesterton, "Why I Am a Catholic" Available online at https://www.chesterton.org/why-i-am-a-catholic/.

154 G.K. Chesterton, "The Surrender Upon Sex" Available online at https://www.americamagazine.org/issue/100/surrender-sex.

Chapter 8

155 James White vs. Peter Stravinskas, "Great Debate VI: Purgatory" May 31, 2001, www.youtube.com/watch?v=PtAkuMs54qM.

156 Diarmaid MacCulloch, *The Reformation: A History* (New York: Viking, 2003), 127.

157 Philip Schaff, *The Creeds of Christendom,* vol. 1 (1877; New York: Cosimo Books, 2007), 175.

158 *Against the Fundamental Epistle of Manichaeus*, 5.

159 Ibid.

160 For a contemporary Protestant defense of this concept see Michael Kruger, *Canon Revisited: Establishing the Origins and Authority of the New Testament Books* (Wheaton, IL: Crossway, 2012).

161 *Against Heresies*, 3.4.1.

162 Philip Schaff, *History of the Christian Church: Modern Christianity/ The German Reformation,* vol. 7 (1882; Grand Rapids, MI: Wm. B. Eerdmans, 1965), 650-53.

163 *Ad Petri Cathedram*, 72.

164 Michael Ivens, *Understanding the Spiritual Exercises* (Leominster, UK: Gracewing, 1998) 260.

165 St. Ignatius goes on to say, "For we believe that between Christ our Lord the bridegroom, and the Church, his bride, there is the same Spirit who governs and directs us for the good of our souls." According to Ivens, "In the formulation of the rule, the term bride and mother and the reference to the Spirit, establish the faith-context within which the rule is to be understood. The black/white antithesis is likely to have been a direct riposte to a statement of Erasmus." Ibid.

166 For more, see Patrick Madrid, *Pope Fiction: Answers to 30 Myths & Misconceptions About the Papacy* (Irving, TX: Basilica Press, 2005), 259-71.

167 Gary Macy, "Pope John XXII," in *An Introductory Dictionary of Theology and Religious Studies,* eds., Orlando O. Espín and James B. Nickoloff (Collegeville, MN:, Liturgical Press, 2007), 684.

168 "Letter to Gregory XI," in *Saint Catherine of Siena as Seen in Her Letters,* trans., Vida D. Scudder (New York: E.P. Dutton & Co., 1905), 185.

169 St. Teresa of Avila, *Interior Castle* trans., E. Allison Peers (New York: Dover Thrift, 2007), 14.

170 G.K. Chesterton, "The Catholic Church and Conversion," in *The Collected Works of G.K. Chesterton,* vol. 3 (San Francisco: Ignatius Press, 1990), 111.

171 *Quo Primum,* www.papalencyclicals.net/pius05/p5quopri.htm.

172 *Treatise 1.*

173 Ibid. In the second edition of this work Cyprian makes this primacy more implicit but still begins what he calls an "easy proof for faith" with Scripture passages about Peter from Matthew 16 and John 21. The Orthodox scholar Nicholas Afanassief says that even though Cyprian believed all the bishops shared one kind of equal authority

NOTES 145

(a position with which Catholics agree), "the place given by [Cyprian] to the Roman Church did raise it above the 'harmonious multitude.'" Nicholas Afanassief, "The Church which Presides in Love", in *The Primacy of Peter: Essays in Ecclesiology and the Early Church*, ed. John Meyendorff (Crestwood, NY: St. Vladimir's Press, 1992), 98.

174 John Henry Cardinal Newman, *An Essay on the Development of Christian Doctrine* (Notre Dame, IN: University of Notre Dame Press, 1994) 3.

Chapter 9

175 "Letter to Mr. John Smith, March 25, 1747," in *The Works of the Rev. John Wesley, A.M.,* vol. 12 (London: Wesleyan Conference Office, 1872), 89.

176 St. John Chrysostom, "Homily 3 on Acts of the Apostles."

177 Trent Horn, *Why We're Catholic: Our Reasons for Faith, Hope, and Love* (El Cajon: Catholic Answers Press, 2017), 219.

178 Alfred Monnin, *Life of the Curé D'Ars* (Baltimore: Kelly and Piet, 1885), 281.

179 "Benedict XVI Pens Prayer for World Rosary Relay," *Zenit,* June 23, 2011, zenit.org/articles/benedict-xvi-pens-prayer-for-world-rosary-relay/.

180 Francis Sweeney, "The Roman Catholic Church—Three Reports on Trouble," *New York Times* April 2, 1972, www.nytimes.com/1972/04/02/archives/out-of-the-curtained-world-the-story-of-an-american-nun-who-left.html?mcubz=1.

181 Louis Antoine Fauvelet de Bourrienne, *Memoirs of Napoleon Bonaparte*, ed., R.W. Phipps, vol. 1 (London: Richard Bentley and Son, 1885), 451.

182 Horn, *Why We're Catholic*, 210.

183 George Craig Stewart, *The Call of Christ* (Milwaukee: Morehouse Publishing Co., 1931), anglicanhistory.org/usa/gcstewart/call1931.html.

184 Abigail Van Buren, "Dear Abby . . . Sinners and Saints!." *Park City Daily News*, April 1, 1964, 5.

185 Penelope Fitzgerald, *The Knox Brothers* (Washington, DC: Counterpoint, 2000), 252.

186 Charles Stanley, *Eternal Security* (Nashville, TN: Thomas Nelson, Inc. 1990), 79.

187 See Volkan Topalli, Timothy Brezina, Mindy Bernhardt, "With God on My Side: The Paradoxical Relationship Between Religious Belief and Criminality among Hardcore Street Offenders," *Theoretical Criminology* 17, no. 1 (October 15, 2012): 49-69.

188 Dietrich Bonhoeffer, *The Cost of Discipleship* (New York: Touchstone, 1995), 48.

189 Ibid., 45.

190 See www.chesterton.org/wrong-with-world/.

191 "Hypocrisy" in *New Dictionary of Christian Ethics & Pastoral Theology*, eds. David J. Atkinson, et. al (Downer's Grove, IL: InterVarsity Press, 2013), 532.

192 Josemaría Escrivá, "The Forge, 169," in *The Way/Furrow/The Forge* (Scepter Publishers, New York, 2001), 608.

193 Nelson Mandela, *Conversations with Myself* (New York: Farrar, Straus & Giroux, 2010), 410.

194 Josemaría Escrivá, *Friends of God* (New York: Scepter Publishers, 2002), Kindle edition.

195 *Two Letters of St. Thérèse of Lisieux to Abbé Bellière.*

Chapter 10

196 Leroy Thompson, *Money Cometh! To the Body of Christ* (Darrow, LA: Ever Increasing Word Ministries, 1996), Kindle edition.

197 Joel Osteen, *Your Best Life Now: 7 Steps to Living at Your Full Potential* (New York: FaithWords, 2014), 228-29.

198 Victoria Osteen, *Love Your Life: Living Happy, Healthy, and Whole* (New York: Free Press, 2008), 55.

198 St. Teresa of Avila, *Interior Castle* (Notre Dame, IN: Ave Maria Press, 2007), 290.

200 Gerald May, M.D., *Addiction and Grace: Love and Spirituality in the Healing of Addictions* (New York: HarperOne, 2007), 17.

201 Ibid., 18.

202 *Confessions*, Book I, Part I.

203 St. Francis de Sales was the spiritual director of Bishop Jean-Pierre Camus, who credits his mentor as saying, "Be patient with everyone, but above all with yourself. I mean do not be disheartened by your imperfections, but always rise up with fresh courage." Jean-Pierre Camus, *The Spirit of St. Francis de Sales,* trans., H.L. Sydney Lear (London: Rivingtons, 1887), 220.

204 Michael LeBoeuf, *Imagineering: How to Profit from Your Creative Powers* (Chicago: Contemporary Books, 1980), 157. Thanks to Father Horton for pointing me in the right direction toward the original attribution. "St. Francis de Sales: Your value as a human being," Fauxtations.wordpress.com, January 24, 2017, fauxtations.wordpress.com/2017/01/24/st-francis-de-sales-your-worth-as-a-human-being/.

205 The oldest might be the story of King Midas, who wished that everything he touched would turn to gold, forgetting that his touch also affected what he ate and drank. In some versions, he turned his daughter into a golden statue.

206 In the original text Capote says "Saint Thérèse," but the book's editor believes this was a mistake on the part of the original publisher and is certain Capote meant St. Teresa of Avila. Truman Capote, *Answered Prayers* (New York: Random House, 2012), xv.

207　Ibid, 18.

208　Teresa of Avila, *The Book of Her Life,* trans., Kieran Kavanaugh and Otilio Rodriguez (Indianapolis, IN: Hackett Publishing, 2008), 82.

209　*Autobiography,* Manuscript 25C. In the original text Thérèse wrote, *"Pour moi, la prière, c'est un élan du coeur, c'est un simple regard jeté vers le Ciel, c'est un cri de reconnaissance et d'amour au sein de l'*épreuve *comme au sein de la joie."*

210　Fr. John Zuhlsdorf, "St. Augustine: 'He who sings prays twice,'" Fr. Z's Blog, February 20, 2006, wdtprs.com/blog/2006/02/st-augustine-he-who-sings-prays-twice/.

211　*General Instruction of the Roman Missal,* 39.

212　St. John of the Cross, *The Collected Works of St. John of the Cross,* trans., Kieran Kavanaugh and Otilio Rodriguez (Washington, DC: ICS Publications, 2017), 92.

213　"Address of His Holiness Benedict XVI to the German Pilgrims Who Had Come to Rome for the Inauguration Ceremony of the Pontificate," April 25, 2005, w2.vatican.va/content/benedict-xvi/en/speeches/2005/april/documents/hf_ben-xvi_spe_20050425_german-pilgrims.html, cited in Mark Giszczak, "Were You Made for Greatness or for God?," Catholic Bible Student.com, February 17, 2014, catholicbiblestudent.com/2014/02/greatness-god.html.

214　*Spe Salvi,* 33.

215　*Sermon 19 on the New Testament.*

About the Author

TRENT HORN is a staff apologist for Catholic Answers. He has a master's degree in theology from Franciscan University of Steubenville and is currently pursuing a graduate degree in philosophy from Holy Apostles College. He is the author of four other books: *Why We're Catholic*, *Answering Atheism*, *Persuasive Pro-life*, and *Hard Sayings: A Catholic Approach to Answering Bible Difficulties*.